THE SYMBOL THEORY

Theory, Culture & Society

Theory, Culture & Society caters for the resurgence of interest in culture within contemporary social science and the humanities. Building on the heritage of classical social theory, the book series examines ways in which this tradition has been reshaped by a new generation of theorists. It will also publish theoretically informed analyses of everyday life, popular culture, and new intellectual movements.

EDITOR: Mike Featherstone, *Teesside Polytechnic*

EDITORIAL BOARD
Roy Boyne, *Newcastle-upon-Tyne Polytechnic*
Mike Hepworth, *University of Aberdeen*
Scott Lash, *University of Lancaster*
Roland Robertson, *University of Pittsburgh*
Bryan S. Turner, *University of Essex*

Also in this series

The Body
Social Process and Cultural Theory
edited by Mike Featherstone, Mike Hepworth and Bryan S. Turner

Consumer Culture and Postmodernism
Mike Featherstone

Talcott Parsons
Theorist of Modernity
edited by Roland Robertson and Bryan S. Turner

Religion and Social Theory
Second edition
Bryan S. Turner

Images of Postmodern Society
Social Theory and Contemporary Cinema
Norman K. Denzin

Promotional Culture
Advertising, Ideology and Symbolic Expression
Andrew Wernick

THE SYMBOL THEORY

Norbert Elias

edited with an introduction by
Richard Kilminster

S SAGE Publications
London • Newbury Park • New Delhi

This edition first published 1991

'The Symbol Theory: An Introduction' originally appeared
in three parts in *Theory, Culture & Society*, 6 (2, 3 and 4)
(1989), pp. 169–217, 339–383 and 499–537

 SAGE Publications Ltd
6 Bonhill Street
London EC2A 4PU

SAGE Publications Inc
2455 Teller Road
Newbury Park, California 91320

SAGE Publications India Pvt Ltd
32, M-Block Market
Greater Kailash – I
New Delhi 110 048

Published in association with *Theory, Culture & Society*,
Department of Administrative and Social Studies, Teesside
Polytechnic

British Library Cataloguing in Publication data

Elias, Norbert
  The symbol theory.
  I. Title
  301.01

  ISBN 0–8039–8418–9
  ISBN 0–8039–8419–7 pbk

Library of Congress catalog card number 90–62092

Typeset by Photoprint, Torquay
Printed in Great Britain by Dotesios Ltd,
Trowbridge, Wiltshire

CONTENTS

EDITOR'S INTRODUCTION

Richard Kilminster

Un problème convenablement posé est bien près
d'être résolu.

(André Marie Ampère,
quoted in Bravo 1979: 204)

The Symbol Theory turned out to be the last extended work to be completed for publication by Norbert Elias during his lifetime. He died on 1 August 1990 in Amsterdam, at the age of 93. This book reproduces as one text, but otherwise unchanged, his wide-ranging study 'The Symbol Theory: An Introduction', which originally appeared in three instalments in successive issues of *Theory, Culture and Society* during 1989. The picture by Paul Klee on the cover of this book had been chosen by Elias for this purpose shortly before he died. But sadly he was still working on a new Introduction in the days just before his death. In consultation with the publishers and the Norbert Elias Foundation, it was decided that this poignant document should be published in its unfinished state. It is therefore included below, at the beginning of the text which it was, in its final form, intended to introduce. It breaks off in mid-stream, with Elias in a characteristically expansive mood, beginning to develop a discussion of one of his favourite themes: the need to study human societies on a very long timescale. We can only guess at the direction the rest of the argument might have taken.

The main text went through various phases before attaining its present shape. Like all Elias's writings in the later years, it was dictated to an assistant. It was originally completed in this way in draft in the summer of 1988. The copious, unsectioned and rather repetitive manuscript formed a continuous flow of interlocking themes. I fashioned a more structured, and hence accessible, text for publication in the journal by inserting paragraphs, eliminating unnecessary repetitions and arranging the sequence of numbered sections, which he had begun but not sustained.

In doing the original editing I found myself following closely a sequence of themes and argumentation that was already present in the material. Despite the repetition, the manuscript seemed to fall naturally into a pattern, which I was fortunate in being able to discuss with Elias. Because he was unable to read back through the pages as he composed and revised them, due to his failing eyesight, Elias had to carry the whole framework of this work in his head as he proceeded. It was all the more remarkable, therefore, to discover how systematic and structured the seemingly formless manuscript actually was. All my deletions and re-orderings were agreed with him and he rewrote some shorter sections. At his insistence, however, some repetitious passages had to be left in and readers may find these irksome in the unchanged text. But, as I point out later, there is a fine line between these passages and what one might call Elias's benign repetitions, which are a characteristic of his style generally, whereby he tends to return to the same issues several times, reworking them on each occasion in different ways.

The Symbol Theory is a vintage example of Elias's later *oeuvre*, but readers unfamiliar with his work who come cold to this book might find its mode of presentation and terminology strange compared with the more usual professional academic product. A few guidelines and pointers for reading his highly original writings generally might therefore be helpful for approaching this one.

For most of his long career, for reasons often beyond his control, Elias was on the periphery of the sociology establishment and thus distanced from it. He therefore felt few of the pressures of the institutionalized world of the academic social sciences.[1] Hence, what the reader will not find in any of Elias's books or articles — and in this respect *The Symbol Theory* is typical — is the customary beginning with a review of the literature or contemporary debates about the problem or topic addressed, in this case symbols. Elias did not work that way. Rather, he always went for the problem or object of inquiry (for example, scientific establishments, Mozart, time, violence, Freud, ageing and dying, work, psychosomatics, to name just a few of the other subjects he investigated in recent years), which he would explore in his own way. The efforts of others working in different ways and within different sociological traditions in the field were of secondary interest to him. He left to his readers the task of ascertaining the compatibility with his own paradigm of concepts and findings developed elsewhere.

A lengthy and discursive Elias article will, therefore, typically have very few references cited; indeed, frequently there will only be one, perhaps to an obscure book published many years ago. *The Symbol Theory* is no exception, containing just one reference, to a book by Julian Huxley from 1941 on the issue of the evolutionary uniqueness of man. If you complained to Elias that he had failed to address the contemporary literature, or suggested that he was out of date, he would reply that you had a fetish for the new: that just because a book is old it does not mean that it may not still be the best treatment of a problem. And conversely, new books did not necessarily represent an advance simply because they were new. It was the intrinsic cognitive worth of the book that counted, not whether it was currently *à la mode*.[2] He was oblivious to intellectual fads and fashions, working within a scientific timescale, a breadth of vision and a level of detachment which can only be described as Olympian.

Elias had a joyful and insatiable scientific curiosity about the world. He often described the vocation of the sociologist as one of embarking on a 'voyage of discovery' into the largely unknown realm of society. He himself always navigated with the aid of his own theories and in his own language of figurational or 'process' sociology, as he began to call it towards the end of his life. For Elias, his was the primary paradigm in the sociological arena and he had right of way, but not in any inflexible, dogmatic sense. No one could have been more open to the empirical counter-example and to dialogue than he. But it was simply that he possessed an unshakeable conviction in the originality and importance of his work as a synthesis and as a research programme. He was very sure about what he was doing. He could always point to the demonstrable explanatory power of the sociological models he had developed in *The Civilizing Process* (1978–82; in German 1939) and *The Court Society* (1983; in German 1969) and draw upon his vast knowledge of history and the sciences, in which he had few contemporary equals.

Johan Goudsblom has pointed out that in Elias's earlier works from the 1930s there is in fact a good deal more implicit theoretical and methodological polemic with other authors and schools than is immediately apparent. In his later writings this engagement became more explicit, with Elias critically taking on a number of named writers (Goudsblom 1987). This is true, though the implicit mode of polemic can take another form, which we find in this book. He also favoured criticizing other approaches to a problem in a broader, more allusive way, as exemplifying styles of thought or characteristic paradigms. He might allude to, say, the shortcomings of 'action theory', 'Marxist theory', 'phenomenology' or, as here, to 'traditional theories of knowledge'. His critique would in-variably find them fatally flawed by reductionism, individualism, over-abstraction, philosophical hangovers, covert political senti-ments (a kind of 'involvement' in Elias's terminology) or various combinations thereof. But in general he never got caught up excessively in the cut-and-thrust of the contemporary debates and elaborate in-house discussions that go on in sociology. He believed that the progress of the discipline was best served by theoretically-informed empirical research; but it was greatly hindered by sociologists expending their energies on the controversies of the time or on debating with each other.

It is worth mentioning the style of Elias's writings. Wolf Lepenies (1978: 63) aptly described their qualities: 'a jargon-free concern with clarity, a careful training in sociological observation and a thorough-going combination of theoretical discussions with often surprising references to details.' Elias is also often provocative and challenging and he revelled in citing hallowed but defunct dualisms and subjecting to scrutiny what seems obvious. He does all these things in this book as he talks about the relationship between human thinking and communication and the evolution of biological nature. Elias convinces readers, not so much by conven-tional 'logical' arguments for this or that position, as by expressing issues in such a way as to provoke people into reflecting upon the categories or assumptions that they routinely employ in dealing with them. Having read *The Symbol Theory* it is hard, for example, ever again to use unreflectively the oppositions of idealism/materialism and nature/culture or to succumb to the fallacious temptation of regarding language as existing in an independent realm of its own.

Echoes of the German sociology of knowledge reverberate in this piece, as in much of Elias's work. But he took the tradition much further, deepening and extending that part of the programme which called for a sociological epistemology and ontology to replace traditional philosophy. It is the trace in Elias's project of this tradition that accounts for another characteristic of his style. Very often he explores a problem first by exposing the static dichotomies involved in customary approaches, and then returning to them several times whilst expounding a wider and more inclusive alternative framework of explanation. This framework proves to be, of course, his own sociology of figurations, developed out of his work on civilizing processes. It is always from this standpoint that Elias writes. Some, though by no means all, of the repetitions in this book are explicable by this organic feature of his mode of argumentation.

Elias's mode of discussion, then, effectively transposes on to another level the problems as originally posed. As they are absorbed into the wider sociological framework, the traditional (often philosophical) ways of talking about the issue are then exposed as simply untenable. In this book we can follow Elias in this strategy through the traditional oppositions of idealism/ materialism, matter/spirit, nature/culture, form/content and consciousness/being. In particular, the limitations of the subject/ object dualism recur and Elias sociologically traces this opposition back to the indubitable self-experience of people as *homo clausus* characteristic of societies (notably in the West) that have attained a far-reaching phase of a civilizing process. The crusade against this model of human beings is indeed one of the most dominant themes in Elias's work.

For all the reasons so far mentioned, I think it is important to read this book right through several times in order to get the best out of it. Not only was Elias one of those writers in the German tradition who lay very great stress on the importance of the way in which you pose a question, but also he was very alert to the nuances and associations of the language and concepts we employ in sociology, which is a related sensitivity. His call to us to unlearn older categories in order to develop a more detached and realistic image of human beings within an evolutionary framework and timescale — which is partly what this book is about — is, however, neither an easy nor a solely 'rational' task. It inevitably involves people having to change the picture they have of themselves, perhaps in a direction that is uncomfortable. Elias evoked the bleak force of his evolutionary image of humankind in a stanza from his poem 'Riding the Storm' (Elias 1988: 81):

> born from a storm of disorder
> nomads of time without tiding
> in a void without border
> riding the storm

The process of re-forming our image of human beings obviously
entails overcoming emotional hurdles. This struggle is part of what
Elias elsewhere called the sociological problem of how far and
under what conditions people are capable of 'facing themselves'
(Elias 1987a: 12–14, 39–40). Already one can detect a difference
of substance between this conception and the more familiar,
rationalistic dictum of 'know thyself'. It was with some under-
statement that Mike Featherstone (1987: 201) correctly commented
that Elias 'demands a great deal from the reader'.

More specifically, how does *The Symbol Theory* fit into the
corpus of Elias's works? One message carried in all his writings,
as a cautionary tale for sociologists, is that seemingly disparate
social events and processes, analysed and artificially separated by
the various professionally organized social science establishments
and by specialisms within sociology, are in fact all aspects of the
same interwoven societal process. His writings, too, form a
seamless web. Like a number of other social scientists, however,
Elias had noticed the explanatory usefulness of the concept of
relative autonomy,[3] which he used both to describe the process
whereby human knowledge becomes independent of its original
producers and the way in which specialist social institutions
(economic, political, scientific) become functionally self-sustaining
and bounded in complex societies. This concept also gave Elias
licence, within his synoptic view of the interconnectedness of
social processes, to write on themes, such as sport, sciences, time,
death and dying, various branches of art and artists, and so on.

The Symbol Theory is an exploratory theoretical essay which
brings to the foreground the implications of another relatively
autonomous, interwoven level, the longer-term process of biological
evolution. This process is often relegated by sociologists to the
status of simply the biological background to social life in industrial societies. For Elias, however, a longer-run understanding of
social development needs to be integrated into the overall evolutionary process. As he puts it:

> The natural constitution of human beings prepares them for
> learning from others, for living with others, for being cared for

by others and for caring for others. It is difficult to imagine how social scientists can gain a clear understanding of the fact that nature prepares human beings for life in society without including aspects of the evolutionary process and of the social development of humankind in their field of vision. (p. 145 below)

In discussions, Elias told me that he regarded *The Symbol Theory* as linked with the cluster of his writings on the sociology of knowledge, including *Über die Zeit* (1984), the collection *Involvement and Detachment* (1987a) and various other articles in this area from the 1970s and 1980s (see bibliography). In particular, the fragments 'Reflections on the Great Evolution' (in Elias 1987a) and the article 'On Human Beings and Their Emotions: A Process-Sociological Essay' (Elias 1987b) connect closely with this book. In a very radical programme, Elias establishes the sociology of knowledge in this group of writings as the historical inheritor of the problems of epistemology and ontology of the superseded traditional philosophy of knowledge, which was dominated by a highly individualistic conception of the knowing subject.

He also developed a sociological model of the sciences of a kind that would today be called a realist one, although without the transcendental, philosophical inspiration of much of the current work in this field (Bhaskar 1979). On Elias's model, each science investigates a relatively autonomous level of integration (the physical, the chemical, the biological, the psychological, the social, etc.) of the universe as its 'object', to use the terminology of philosophers. This model — which he pointedly calls a science of sciences — (Elias 1974) provides a more differentiated, structural conception of the subject matter of the sciences, and hence of the differing methods appropriate to them. He offers this model — which posits a hierarchy of sciences — as an empirically usable alternative to working with the subject–object distinction.[4]

For Elias, the social sciences lag behind the natural sciences because of the prevalence within their academic establishments of heteronomous evaluations and emotional involvements, which dominate the character of the knowledge produced. Hence, the human capacity to control social processes lags behind the capacity to control natural processes, because in the natural sciences the balance long ago shifted further over into the predominance of autonomous evaluations, signifying a breakthrough to greater detachment (Elias 1987a).

One prominent polemical target for Elias in this group of writings is the Kantian conception of the *a priori*, which he criticizes relentlessly from an empirical–sociological point of view. Neither will he have any truck with nominalists, individualists and phenomenologists, nor reductionists of any kind — economic, physicalistic, or biologistic. These polemics recur in Elias's works on the sociology of knowledge in particular and are also found in various combinations in *The Symbol Theory*.

In this book the programmatic focus is on evolutionary biology as a human science to be woven, in a non-reductive manner, into a longer-term conception of human development, consistent with the theory of levels of integration. It is obvious from the text that for Elias evolutionary theory is not to be identified solely with Darwin's version, which he clearly regards as incomplete and representing an early stage of elaboration. I think that also on Elias's agenda is the intention to steer between the two extreme ideological positions which commonly permeate research on the animalic dimension of human beings. On the one hand lies the reductionist view of the ethologists and sociobiologists such as E.O. Wilson and others (Segerstrale 1986), which effectively says that we are basically apes. On the other hand is the philosophical–religious view that human beings constitute a complete break with the animal world, forming a level of soul or spirit. As I read him, Elias is trying theoretically to clear the decks for developing a new model of humankind to deal with these and other related questions, which usually tend to be posed only in such one-sided and evaluative ways.

The 'Great Evolution' provides the synthetic framework for all the sciences, including sociology. Anticipating the accusations of evolutionary determinism or teleology, he draws the crucial distinction here, as in several other places in this group of writings, between largely irreversible biological *evolution* and potentially reversible social *development*. The life cycle of stars and the development of societies are not of the same kind: unlike a star, it is possible for a society to go into reverse and revert back to an earlier stage, say to feudal social relations. With this point in mind, Elias usually talked of civilizing and *decivilizing* processes together. Within this great framework of socio-natural development, Elias sees the technical human capacity for communication via symbols to be a unique achievement of the blind inventiveness of nature. The capacity of humans to steer their conduct by means of learned knowledge gave them a great evolutionary advantage over other species which were unable to accomplish this at all or only to a very limited extent. He calls this humankind's 'symbol emancipation' (p. 53). Hence the survival of human groups has been to an important degree dependent upon object-congruent knowledge. For Elias, there are vital lessons to be learned from this realization for the future of humankind in the next stages of its development.

The aim of the research programme opened up in *The Symbol Theory* is to provide a more adequate socio-biological picture of the human capacity for symbol formation than is possible with theories that employ or imply the static nature/culture and abstract/concrete polarities, which contain dualistic, metaphysical undertones. Working with such polarities would blind us to grasping symbol formation as a process of *advancing synthesis*, a key term which covers the demonstrable fact that concepts have embedded within them traces of previous stages of social and scientific development. He therefore prefers this concept to the more customary and static term abstraction. To put these matters in another way, Elias is interested in establishing the mode of existence of symbols, as learned means of communication, in a diachronic manner in an evolutionary framework which includes social development as its continuation on a higher level.

It might be instructive to illustrate the idea of advancing synthesis from Elias's writings on time and timing (Elias 1982, 1984) to supplement the discussion given in the text. Elias shows that the concept of time is a pre-eminent example of a concept of high-level synthesis, a learned symbol which enables people to relate two sequences of events in different levels of integration to each other, by using one sequence as the timing yardstick for the other one. It is not simply an abstraction or a capacity of the mind, nor is it a universal substance, as philosophers have variously claimed, but is a concept which has developed under specific conditions and serves to aid people's orientation. People in less differentiated societies have a different time experience and often have no need for personal timepieces. The discernible development is from a more personalized, discontinuous conception of time in simpler societies to a more impersonal and continuous conception in the more complex state societies, corresponding to the lengthening of chains of interdependencies and functional differentiation. In the latter societies, highly self-controlled people have to adjust themselves to each other as part of an increasingly intricate mesh of contacts and social necessities, which requires a socially standardized, high-level symbol of timing to enable this to be done with great accuracy and predictability.

As I mentioned earlier, as something of an outsider to the sociology establishment, Elias was never bothered much about such professional niceties as beginning any of his writings with the customary review of the literature in the field, or situating his work in relation to the writings of others in any systematic way. He was much more interested in developing and extending his own theories. Inevitably, he left behind the problem of ascertaining the compatibility of his legacy with the work of others and with recent findings in the fields he entered. In the case of this book how, if at all, is Elias's exploratory theoretical work affected by recent developments in the theory of biological evolution? Or by studies of the human symbolizing capacity found in the work of anthropologists? Elias was working towards a synthesis of all the sciences, for which, if it is to be achieved by those who follow him, it will be necessary to sift the recent findings of various disciplines to an extent that he was either unable or unwilling to do. There is a lot of work to be done testing the strength of Elias's theoretical reflections in this way. In the above two fields alone, the literature is obviously vast and such a task cannot be attempted here. All I can do in practice is to contrast Elias's research programme in *The Symbol Theory* in very general terms with some prominent approaches found elsewhere, in order to begin the process. I can only cite for the sake of comparison a few exemplars within the range of my knowledge and competence.

Anthropologists and sociologists, past and present, who have investigated symbols have tended to focus on their function in social cohesion and rituals (Durkheim [1914] 1968; Turner 1967, 1969; Firth 1975; Augé 1982) or in social boundary maintenance (Douglas 1966). Elias's work does not address either of these two problems directly, though they could, I think, be considerably illuminated by being addressed in an Eliasian manner. Philosophers, structuralists and semiologists have been concerned with the relationship between the symbol and what it stands for (Cassirer 1953; Eco 1984). Elias's interest could be seen as being closer to that of the latter group, in that he shares, as a perceived problem, their parallel discovery of the links between language, knowing and thinking, a theme central to this book. But Elias had already long ago decisively distanced himself from the latent (or sometimes not so latent) Kantianism which pervades much of this research, particularly the later work inspired by Claude Lévi-Strauss. Elias also importantly re-evaluates the philosophical concept of 'meaning' which is implied in this approach (in section III). More than them, too, Elias stresses the emotions which are bound up in symbolization and he has a dynamic, developmental orientation in contrast to the synchronic cast of much structuralist research.

The crucial difference, however, between all this work and that of Elias in this book, is that Elias insists that symbols are also tangible sound patterns of human communication and hence also 'physical' data, made possible by the evolutionary biological precondition of the unique and complex vocal apparatus of humans. This feature enables them to make a wide variety of sounds and hence to produce many group-specific languages. The situating of the problem within an evolutionary framework in this particular way makes Elias's efforts unique among contemporary sociological approaches to symbol formation. Some anthropologists — who have been able generally to develop a greater degree of detachment in their inquiries than that so far achieved by sociologists — are also moving in this direction (Borchert and Zihlman 1990). For many contemporary sociologists, however, the dominant paradigms currently available are either rather narrowly 'culturalist' or discourse-oriented (Mulkay 1985) or crudely causal and interests-reductive (Bloor 1976). Elias offers a real alternative (Wassall 1990).

Regarding symbols also as tangible sound patterns additionally enables Elias to avoid the rationalistic temptation of assuming that symbol systems are part of an independent realm of culture with a reality of its own. The existence of this temptation is no mere logical possibility. Consider Jeffrey Alexander's comment: 'Recent developments in cultural studies converge in their emphasis on the autonomy of culture from social structure' (1990: 25). Elias's discussions in this book were not, as far as I know, a direct response to the extensive current debates in sociology about culture (Archer 1988; Robertson 1990; Arnason 1987; Alexander 1990), even though his approach can illuminate them in surprising ways. With their different stances and for their differing purposes, many of these writers also address questions about the origins and functioning of symbol systems and readers will need to make their

own comparisons with the much longer-term evolutionary framework employed in this book. Elias addresses head-on a question
which is often fudged in these debates: what is the ontological
status of knowledge? The subtlety with which he tackles this
matter sociologically and dynamically, moving beyond the traditional alternatives of idealism or materialism, makes fascinating
reading (see section V on cerebral memory images). Elias over-
comes the traditional nature/culture and structure/culture dualisms
by dipping them into the stream of continuity from the evolution
of the human species through to the development of human
societies as a level of integration in its own right.

For Elias, then, the human condition is embedded within social
developments which continue the blind evolutionary process on to
another level. Symbol formation is bound up with human survival
in this process. This vision shares a good deal, in general terms,
with that of an earlier generation of evolutionists who, in the 1940s
and 1950s, established what is usually called the Modern Synthesis
in the theory of evolution (Futuyma 1986: ch. 1) upon which Elias
largely draws. It is no accident that a book by Julian Huxley from
1941 is the only one cited by Elias here. Elias already knew the
biological sciences quite well from his early training in medicine
in Germany in the 1920s, but there is a special affinity between
the conception of biological evolution found in *The Symbol
Theory* and that embodied in the work of writers such as Julian
Huxley, Joseph Needham, C.H. Waddington and others, whose
work Elias must have encountered in its heyday, during the forty-
year period when he lived, taught and researched in Britain
(approximately 1935–75).

Although not a unified school as such, all these writers shared
the view that society is an emergent phenomenon, irreducible to
the previous physical, chemical and biological levels. What Elias
calls the social 'level of integration' was variously described by
these earlier evolutionists as the social 'level of organization'
(Needham 1944); the 'field of psychosocial integration' (Reiser
1958); and the phase of 'psycho-social evolution' (Huxley 1942,
1953).[5] Needham even called his theory one of 'integrative levels'.
Like Elias they, too, were concerned to establish human beings as
an evolutionary breakthrough, a progression from a lower to a
higher form, which Huxley and others called an example of
anagenesis (Waddington 1961). Other common ground includes

the conception of higher levels of integration as canalizing the lower ones; the importance of knowledge transmission and learning in human development; the uniqueness of the human capacity for symbolization; the issue of how humans might now come to guide the evolutionary process from their position as its highest level; and the need to look forward towards global trends which might be leading towards the self-integration of humankind into a world civilization (Huxley 1961).

We do not know from the published writings and correspondence of Elias to date how much of the detail of the Modern Synthesis he accepted and what he rejected, nor even if he was aware of the consensus. Nor whether he was conversant with current developments in the field relating to random genetic drift, survival of genes as well as groups of relatives, populations and species (Futuyma 1986: 13). Nor whether he thought these significantly affected his version of evolutionary theory. All these questions need to be asked by investigators wishing to follow the lead laid down in *The Symbol Theory*. I am suggesting only the affinity.

But it is clear that whilst Elias draws much from these writers, he also departs from them because of the staunchly sociological way in which he handles the issues. He has a highly developed sociologist's sense of the way in which people's ideological or disciplinary biases can significantly shape their observations of biological realities. And he puts much more emphasis on explaining the direction of successive integrative/disintegrative stages of social development, within the overall social level of integration, than did any of the evolutionary biologists. His terminology for dealing with this level is noticeably tighter, more differentiated and adequate to its contours. There is an obvious looseness, for example, in Huxley's term 'phase of psycho-social evolution'. This kind of phrase was appropriate to what he and others were trying to do, that is, simply to establish the irreducibility of the highest human social level to the lower ones, as part of an ethical–humanistic world-view based on an evolutionary picture of humankind.

For Elias, however, before one can reliably get on to that kind of project one has to do a lot of sociological work to control for the intrusion of emotionally charged ideological evaluations into our observations of the biological and social levels of human beings. He sometimes referred to this strategy as the 'detour via detachment' (Elias 1987a: 105–6). It goes hand-in-hand with a long-term perspective on social development. Elias apparently took from the evolutionists of the Modern Synthesis only what he needed to provide the longer-term evolutionary complement to his theories of civilizing processes, scientific differentiation and symbol formation. A few writers — pupils or followers of Elias — have begun to take up his challenge to go for the very long view of social and scientific development (Goudsblom, Jones and Mennell 1989; Wassall 1990), but in the current sociology of science one only finds the odd contribution of a developmental kind of any sort (Hull 1988).

Elias rarely engages in methodological polemics for their own sake. In his later writings he drew attention to the emerging integration of social groups on a global level, which process necessitates extending the scope of sociology beyond the level of integration of the nation-state to that of humankind as a whole, as a bulwark against the intrusion of national self-images into concept formation (Elias 1987c; Mennell 1989: ch. 9). *The Symbol Theory* contributes to this vital extension of scope by situating the investigation of human symbol formation in the very long evolutionary timescale of the human species and showing how it is bound up with communication, orientation and group survival. It thus helps to set a sociological agenda for generating social scientific knowledge appropriate in scope and level of detachment to understanding — and thus potentially aiding survival in — the next phase of humankind's development on that global level, which is emerging all around us. It is intended to provide sociologists with a more realistic and reliable image of humankind as a whole with which to work.

The conceptual ground-clearing exercises and polemics that go on in this book are all partly designed to contribute to this practical goal by trying to eliminate some of the concepts, dualisms and outdated presuppositions mentioned earlier which, if used exclusively, would not provide an adequate understanding for our orientation in the next emerging integrative level. In the hands of entrenched academic establishments, and often tinged with implicit ideological and other evaluations, these abstractions may also represent a higher degree of involvement. As such, they could also contribute more to disorientation and possibly even to the dangerous raising of social tensions during the reintegration transitions towards larger survival units, through which humankind is probably, though by no means inevitably, about to pass.

In the introductory fragment — the last thing he wrote — Elias is still devoting considerable space to criticizing yet again the Kantian *a priori* and Cartesian–Husserlian doubt. This is a task which he had originally embarked upon seventy years before as a postgraduate student under Richard Hönigswald in Breslau! It is tempting to dismiss his continual return to these themes as simply indicating that he was obsessed with them or living in the past, or both. But he had in fact read the important recent developments in Kantian thinking of, for example, Karl-Otto Apel and Jürgen Habermas. Beneath the surface of their new focus on language and on speech communities, he discerned the same transcendental structure of thinking that characterizes all Kantian philosophy.[6] The question remains, though: why did he continue his crusade against this and other rationalist philosophies with undiminished energy until the very end of his life?

The answer lies in the point about orientation just made. What I think galvanized Elias was the realization that the transcendental dimension of Kantian thinking is defeatist. It assumes that people cannot adapt themselves to different situations and develop new ways of thinking from the nature of the emerging new objects they confront: they are forever shackled by fixed categories. And the versions of Cartesian doubt abdicate responsibility completely from the same task, assuming that in the end we can never be sure anyway of the existence of the real world we are trying to grasp. Both philosophies are individualistic and both fly in the face of the evidence of the advancing syntheses historically developed in the sciences in the light of new observations. He maintains that the evidence suggests that there is in fact no limit to the number of symbols and languages that people have created over the centuries and will continue to create.

Elias says towards the end of the introductory fragment that these philosophies, which cast doubt on the existence of anything independent of the knower, are 'the worm in the apple of modernity' (p. 15). They constitute a destructive accompaniment to the scientific movement and can only hinder the crucial cognitive–orientational tasks facing humankind in the next phase of its development. Elias's relentless pursuit of them was no mere vendetta. There was a lot more at stake.

Notes

I would like to thank Stephen Barr, Rudolf Knijff, Terry Wassall and Cas Wouters for their help in preparing this Introduction.

1 For accounts of Elias's life, the publication history of *The Civilizing Process*, the long-delayed recognition of his work in European countries during the 1970s and 1980s and the extensive research in figurational sociology in the Netherlands, see Goudsblom 1977; Lepenies 1978; Korte 1988; Mennell 1989: ch. 1; and Kranendonk 1990.

2 Elias made these points in different ways in various places, but see especially Elias 1987a: 117–18 and 1987c.

3 Elias employs the concept of relative autonomy quite a lot in his writings, particularly those on the sociology of knowledge and sciences. In the history of sociology it has also been found useful by at least Durkheim [1914] 1968: 271; Lukács [1920] 1973: 11; Althusser 1965: 111, 240; Sartre 1968: 80 and Alexander 1990: 1–27. In the British context the concept has come into currency via post-structuralist writings, notably those of Louis Althusser, who used it in his adaptations of the Marxist theory of base and superstructure to avoid economic reductionism. One writer who has consistently refused to separate culture and structure in a rigid, dualistic way, is Zygmunt Bauman (1972, 1973).

4 In the extensive bibliography of the investigations undertaken within the figurational research programme inspired by Elias in the Netherlands (Kranendonk 1990), there is, oddly, only one recorded article specifically on Elias's sociology of knowledge and sciences (Wilterdink 1977). This neglect is out of proportion to the importance Elias obviously attached to this field in his overall output. Probably unique, therefore, is Terence J. Wassall's (1990) unpublished study of Elias's ontology, which argues for an Eliasian developmental approach to the sociology of scientific knowledge to counter the dominant relativistic–constructivist paradigm. He also suggests that Elias has not drawn the most radical conclusions that are possible from his theory of levels of integration and conception of object-adequacy, for understanding the environmental consequences of scientific interventions into the natural world.

5 Although not referring to Elias's writings, C.H. Waddington preferred Elias's key term 'sociogenetic' to describe the cumulative mechanism of social learning: ' "Psychosocial" is Huxley's word. To my mind, it suffers from some redundancy, since the social can hardly avoid being psychological. I prefer to use "sociogenetic", which emphasizes the importance of the mechanism as a means of transmitting information from one generation to the next, which is the crucial point' (Waddington 1961: 74).

6 In a letter to me dated 18.1.81, Elias wrote: 'There are all kinds of contradictions in Apel's approach. He tries to include into his transcendentalism social data, which is simply not possible because social data presuppose a plurality of human beings, while the term "transcendental" refers to givens which a single individual possesses all by himself prior to all experiences.' See also Elias 1982: 24 and further critiques of transcendentalism in Kilminster 1982 and 1989.

Bibliography

Alexander, Jeffrey C. (1990) 'Analytic Debates: Understanding the Relative

Autonomy of Culture', in Jeffrey C. Alexander and Steven Seidman (eds), *Culture and Society: Contemporary Debates*. Cambridge: Cambridge University Press

Althusser, Louis (1965) *For Marx*. London: Allen Lane/Penguin Press (1970)

Archer, Margaret S. (1988) *Culture and Agency: The Place of Culture in Social Theory*. Cambridge: Cambridge University Press

Arnason, Johann (1987) 'Figurational Sociology as a Counter-Paradigm', *Theory, Culture and Society*, 4 (2–3), pp. 429–456

Augé, Marc (1982) *The Anthropological Circle: Symbol, Function, History*, tr. M. Thom. Cambridge: Cambridge University Press

Bauman, Zygmunt (1972) 'Praxis: The Controversial Culture–Society Paradigm', in Teodor Shanin (ed.), *The Rules of the Game: Cross-Disciplinary Essays on Models in Scholarly Thought*. London: Tavistock

Bauman, Zygmunt (1973) *Culture as Praxis*. London: Routledge

Bhaskar, Roy (1979) *The Possibility of Naturalism*. Brighton: Harvester Press

Bloor, David (1976) *Knowledge and Social Imagery*. London: Routledge

Borchert, Catherine M. and Zihlman, Adrienne L. (1990) 'The Ontogeny and Phylogeny of Symbolizing', in Mary Le Cron Foster and Lucy Jayne Botscharow (eds), *The Life of Symbols*, Boulder, Col./Oxford: Westview Press

Bravo, Mario Gian (1979) *Les socialistes avant Marx*, vol. I. Paris: Maspéro

Cassirer, Ernst (1953) *The Philosophy of Symbolic Forms*. New Haven, Conn.: Yale University Press

Douglas, Mary (1966) *Purity and Danger*. London: Routledge

Durkheim, Émile ([1914] 1968) *The Elementary Forms of the Religious Life*. London: George Allen & Unwin

Eco, Umberto (1984) *Semiotics and the Philosophy of Language*. London: Macmillan

Elias, Norbert (1970) 'The Sociology of Knowledge: New Perspectives', *Sociology*, V (2 & 3), pp. 149–168, 355–370

Elias, Norbert (1972) 'Theory of Science and History of Science: Comments on a Recent Discussion', *Economy and Society*, 1 (2), pp. 117–133

Elias Norbert (1974) 'The Sciences: Towards a Theory', in Richard Whitley (ed.), *Social Processes of Scientific Development*. London: Routledge

Elias, Norbert (1978–82) *The Civilizing Process*, 2 vols. Oxford: Basil Blackwell (in German 1939)

Elias, Norbert (1982) 'Scientific Establishments', in Norbert Elias, Herminio Martins and Richard Whitley (eds), *Scientific Establishments and Hierarchies*. Dordrecht/London: Reidel

Elias, Norbert (1983) *The Court Society*. Oxford: Basil Blackwell (in German 1969)

Elias, Norbert (1984) *Über die Zeit*. Frankfurt: Suhrkamp

Elias, Norbert (1987a) *Involvement and Detachment*. Oxford: Basil Blackwell

Elias, Norbert (1987b) 'On Human Beings and Their Emotions: A Process-Sociological Essay', *Theory, Culture and Society*, 4 (2–3), pp. 339–361

Elias, Norbert (1987c) 'The Retreat of Sociologists into the Present', *Theory, Culture and Society*, 4 (2–3), pp. 223–247

Elias, Norbert (1988) *Los der Menschen: Gedichte/Nachdichtungen*. Frankfurt: Suhrkamp

Featherstone, Mike (1987) 'Norbert Elias and Figurational Sociology', *Theory, Culture and Society*, 4 (2–3), pp. 197–211

Firth, Raymond (1975) *Symbols: Public and Private*, 2nd impr. London: George Allen & Unwin

Futuyma, Douglas J. (1986) *Evolutionary Biology*, 2nd edn. Sunderland, Mass.: Sinauer Associates

Goudsblom, Johan (1977) 'Responses to Norbert Elias's work in England, Germany, the Netherlands and France', in Peter Gleichmann, Johan Goudsblom and Hermann Korte (eds), *Human Figurations: Essays for Norbert Elias*. Amsterdam: Amsterdams Sociologisch Tijdschrift

Goudsblom, Johan (1987) 'The Sociology of Norbert Elias: Its Resonance and Significance', *Theory, Culture and Society*, 4 (2–3), pp. 326–329

Goudsblom, Johan, Jones, E.L. and Mennell, Stephen (1989) *Human History and Social Process*. Exeter: University of Exeter Press

Hull, David (1988) *Science as a Process: An Evolutionary Account of the Social and Conceptual Development of Science*. Chicago: Chicago University Press

Huxley, Julian (1942) *Evolution: The Modern Synthesis*. London: Allen & Unwin

Huxley, Julian (1953) *Evolution in Action*. London: Chatto & Windus

Huxley, Julian (1961) (ed.) *The Humanist Frame*. London: George Allen & Unwin

Kilminster, Richard (1982) 'Zur Utopiediskussion aus soziologischer Sicht', in Wilhelm Vosskamp (ed.), *Utopieforschung*, Band 1. Stuttgart: J.B. Metzler Verlag

Kilminster, Richard (1989) 'The Limits of Transcendental Sociology', *Theory, Culture and Society*, 6 (4), pp. 655–663

Korte, Hermann (1988) *Über Norbert Elias*. Frankfurt: Suhrkamp

Kranendonk, Willem H. (1990) *Society as Process: A Bibliography of Figurational Sociology in The Netherlands (up to 1989): Sociogenetic and Psychogenetic Studies*. Amsterdam: Publikatiereeks Sociologisch Instituut

Lepenies, Wolf (1978) 'Norbert Elias: An Outsider Full of Unprejudiced Insight', *New German Critique*, 15 (Fall), pp. 57–64

Lukács, Georg ([1920] 1973) 'The Old Culture and the New Culture', in E. San Juan Jr (ed.), *Marxism and Human Liberation*. New York: Delta

Mennell, Stephen (1989) *Norbert Elias: Civilization and the Human Self-Image*. Oxford: Basil Blackwell

Mulkay, Michael (1985) *The Word and the World: Explorations in the Form of Sociological Analysis*. London: George Allen & Unwin

Needham, Joseph (1944) 'Integrative Levels: A Revaluation of the Idea of Progress', in his *Time: The Refreshing River*. London: George Allen & Unwin

Reiser, Oliver L. (1958) *The Integration of Human Knowledge*. Boston: Extending Horizons Press

Robertson, Roland (1990) 'Globality, Global Culture and Images of World Order', in Hans Haferkamp and Neil Smelser (eds), *Social Change and Modernity*. Berkeley: University of California Press

Segerstrale, Ullica (1986) 'Colleagues in Conflict: An *in vivo* Analysis of the Sociobiology Controversy', *Biology and Philosophy*, 1, pp. 53–87

Turner, Victor (1967) *The Forest of Symbols*. Ithaca, NY.: Cornell University Press

Turner, Victor (1969) *The Ritual Process*. Harmondsworth: Penguin

Sartre, Jean-Paul (1968) *Search for a Method*. New York: Vintage Books (in French 1960)

Waddington, C.H. (1961) 'The Human Animal', in Julian Huxley (ed.), *The Humanist Frame*. London: George Allen & Unwin

Wassall, Terence J. (1990) 'The Development of Scientific Knowledge in Relation to the Development of Societies', PhD thesis, University of Leeds

Wilterdink, Nico (1977) 'Norbert Elias's Sociology of Knowledge and its Significance for the Study of the Sciences', in Peter Gleichmann, Johan Goudsblom and Hermann Korte (eds), *Human Figurations: Essays for Norbert Elias*. Amsterdam: Amsterdams Sociologisch Tijdschrift

INTRODUCTION

Many of the problems raised and discussed in this introduction are not problems of conventional sociology as it is today at this relatively early stage of its development. Not only is it difficult at this stage to come to grips with the processual succession where an event cannot come into being if another, earlier, event has not come into being before. Not only, in other words, does sociology require the perception and symbolic representation of processes, but it also requires a full understanding of the fact that the location of events can take place on a sequence of different levels of integration.

Take the orientation in what we call space. It can be represented by concepts such as breadth, depth or length. But at a higher level of integration it can also be represented by the concept 'space', and it is not unlikely that, in the development of humanity, concepts such as length or breadth preceded the higher integration represented by the concept of space. 'Space' again represents an integration at a lower level of conception than the concept 'dimension', which implicitly indicates that space is not the only level of orientation. The discovery that a comprehensive orientation of an event in space requires its determination in time as well was, as one will remember, a significant scientific event. A full location of an event in space is not possible unless it goes hand in hand with its location in time. In fact, if one says 'Einstein discovered that ours is a four-dimensional universe', one does not actually imply that the integration of means of location at the time-and-space level was unknown before Einstein made it explicit. Every change in length is also a change of time. It is difficult to accept the idea that before Einstein no one was ever aware of this fact. One of his merits was that he had the courage to give scientific proof and expression to an obvious fact.

Suppose I am visiting an unknown town, a street plan in my hand. In this case I need not hesitate to distinguish between two modes of existence. The streets, the houses and squares can be classified as really existing. The city plan is a symbolic representation of that reality. In this case one need not doubt the fitness of symbol and reality. The producer of the map may have made mistakes, but by and large one can trust the self-interest of the publishers who have seen to it that mistakes are corrected and that the city plans they sell are accurate symbolic representations of the city's layout. If one uses the relationship between the physical and social unit of a town and the symbolic representation of its layout in the form of a map as a model, one encounters a difficulty which may remain insurmountable as long as one does not face up to it. It may also seem to be too trivial to deserve closer scrutiny. It is not unreasonable to conceptualize the relationship between a town and its map as that between something really existing and something which is merely its symbolic representation. It satisfies the customary inclination of our age to perceive differences as contrasts. Yet the contrast connotation in this case is that between fantasy and reality. The map and the city have a different, but not a contrasting mode of existence. At present even the most differentiated languages are not differentiated enough to equip those who use them as a means of communication with ready-made linguistic symbols of items which are distinguishable without being antagonistic. As merchandise, maps form part of the same level of reality as the town they represent. As symbolic representations of the town, its maps are at the same time set apart from it. People must be able to distance themselves from the physical reality of the town in order to construct and to use such a map; they must, as it were, mentally ascend to a level of synthesis above that of its existence here and now as a heap of matter.

There are several types of symbolic representation. Maps are only one of them. Languages are another. English-speaking persons wishing to make an observation about the night sky may use the sound pattern 'moon'. In their language this sound pattern symbolically represents the largest heavenly body in the night sky. With the help of a wide range of sound patterns such as this human beings are able to communicate with each other. They are able to store knowledge in their memory(ies?) and to transmit it from one generation to another. A very definite form of social standard-ization makes it possible that within the same society the same sound patterns are recognized by all members more or less in the same sense, that is as symbols standing for the same item of knowledge.

Take another example, the word 'virus'. It was invented and standardized when agents smaller than bacilli, causing specific types of illnesses, had been discovered and a common symbol was needed with the help of which people could communicate about the viruses. Without such a common symbol, communication about them was difficult if not impossible. But the need for names is not confined to rare and specialized objects. The most ordinary objects of our everyday life such as buttons, shirts, stairs and bicycles need a standardized symbolic representation if we are to communicate about them. In fact, anything that is not symbolically represented in the language of a language community is not known by its members: they cannot communicate about it with each other.

That applies not only to single words but to whole sentences, to thoughts in general. But the relationship between symbolic representations in the form of sentences and that which they represent is complex. Sentences and, still more, tissues of sentences can fit that which they try to represent wholly or partly. Nor is the need for communicable symbols confined to particular tangible objects. It extends to the whole fund of knowledge of a language community and ultimately of humanity, including functions, situations, processes, and symbols themselves. Thus every known language provides those who use it as means of communication with symbols which enable them to state unequivocally whether statements they address to each other refer to the senders or to the receivers of the message, and whether to them personally or as members of a group. In modern English and all related languages the series of personal pronouns has this function.

The structure of languages is determined by their social function as means of communication. One can assume that all human societies share with each other a common fund of experiences and thus of knowledge. But they differ widely with regard to the content and scope of their knowledge. Hence one may find that the languages of some societies possess symbolic representations of items of knowledge which those of other societies are lacking. Generally one can say that what is without symbolic representation in the language of a society is not known by its members. One may, however, distinguish between different degrees of knowledge. Thus time-experiences, as I have indicated elsewhere,[1] may be known and linguistically represented in one society at a lower, in another at a higher level of synthesis.

1 See Norbert Elias, *Über die Zeit*, 1984 [Frankfurt: Suhrkamp]

Communication by means of symbols, which may differ from society to society, is one of the singularities of humankind. It is founded in the biological organization of human beings. The immense variability of the sound patterns which human beings can produce as means of communication is one of the conditions of the variability of languages. It is also a condition of the growth of knowledge. Without innovatory changes of the sound patterns of a language, innovatory changes of knowledge would not be possible. Among humans different societies can communicate by means of different languages. The same event, the same experience can be represented by different sound symbols. In the languages of humankind one may find a hundred and one different sound symbols for that which in the English language is called 'the moon'. Human beings have this in common with animals, that their manner of communication is predetermined by their natural organization. Human beings are during an early period of their life by nature prepared for learning a language. Humans differ from other living beings in so far as the sound patterns which are their principal means of communication are not characteristic of the whole species but of the society where they grow up. Moreover, these sound patterns which we call languages are not genetically fixated, but human-made and acquired by the individual member of a society during a lengthy process of learning.

One may rightly say that all this is obvious. It is obvious that the first language, a mother tongue, is not inborn but acquired through learning. It is obvious that a language is not a native heritage of humankind but can differ from society to society. Yet these, like many other properties of humans which indicate their uniqueness among living beings, are seldom moved into the centre of contemporary inquiries and discussions. It is one of the fundamental defects of contemporary human sciences, particularly of those which like sociology include the highest possible levels of synthesis, that the basic model of human beings with which they work is confused and confusing. Representatives of the natural sciences assumed their characteristics as sciences in a period in which the properties of nature, as distinct from a playground of spirits, were widely discussed. A measure of consensus had been reached about the distinguishing features of natural compared with supernatural events. No comparable consensus exists about the basic model of human beings with which the sciences work.

As one might expect, they are engaged in an undecided struggle for supremacy among themselves. For a time it was assumed that the science of economics could provide an overall model of human beings, and biologists have never ceased to claim the lead among human sciences for themselves. The inquiry published here may make it easier to see that in all probability none of these human sciences in their existing form can claim to provide the basic information needed for a basic model of human beings.

It is perhaps not easy to fit the short introduction to a symbol theory which follows here into the accepted scheme of the human sciences. It does not fit into the field of biology as it has been presently shaped, and yet it has enough room for the biological aspects of the human existence. It does not fit into the field of psychology as the term is presently understood. The nature of language cannot be properly explored by a type of psychology which is centred on the individual. Nor does it fit into the main stream of sociology which so far neglects the paradigmatic information which the complex 'knowledge, language, memory and thought' requires. Sooner or later it will become necessary to examine critically the presently ruling division of labour among human or social sciences. The old body–soul division stood as godfather to the division between physiology and psychology. The distinction between political science and the science of economics owes something to the stage of development of the division of labour between professional entrepreneurs and professional politicians. As things are, one seems to take it for granted that the internal structure of human sciences such as psychology, sociology, economics and history may change, while the division of sciences according to the present institutions is tacitly accepted as unchangeable. Yet, underlying the present scheme of the social sciences is a concept of human beings which usually remains unexamined and which, if it is examined, proves to be quite inadequate, if not downright misleading.

The problems explored by social scientists and the solutions they discover are built into a groundwork of concepts at a very high level of synthesis about which few if any questions are asked. They are used routinely as if they were the unchanging property of humanity, and in societies such as ours often have the form of a bipolar antithesis such as 'nature and culture', 'body and mind' or 'subject and object'. If nature and culture or nature and society are perceived in this manner, one may find it difficult to follow the argument put forward here. It is, of course, possible that human culture runs counter to human nature. On the other hand, the constitution of humans makes it necessary for them to make their own cultural products specific for their society. Their biological maturation requires supplementation by a process of social learning. If they have no social opportunity for learning a language, their biological readiness for learning it remains unused. Far from being polar opposites, in the human case biological and social processes in order to become effective must interlock.

Moreover, traditional theories of knowledge and of language tend to present the individual act of knowing or of speaking as the starting point of the task they set themselves. Their point of departure is an individual person quite alone in this world who, with a swing of the arm, catches out of nowhere certain items of knowledge, and seeks an answer to the question how these items can fulfil their task of conveying knowledge from one person to others, how it can have a meaning that corresponds to the object of knowledge transmission. How are sound patterns able to carry to the receiver pictures or, in other words, meanings associated with them by the sender? The question agrees with the relevant evidence, and so the answer can be built near to the evidence too.

But first one has to shake off the compelling force of habituation. Custom has habituated people who are on the look-out for this kind of explication to search for an answer which has the character of a beginning. Such an answer is not to be found. The growth of a language, like that of knowledge, is a continuous process without an absolute break. What one can expect to find in the long run, in other words, is a ceaseless flow of language and of knowledge carrying standardized means of communication and orientation. It is kept alive by standardizing techniques which may or may not be recognized as such. The ability to control patterns of knowledge and speech in a society is usually a concomitant of the distribution of power chances in a society. Spurts of integration and disintegration usually leave traces in the development of a society's language and knowledge.

Theories of knowledge whose central model is a subject–object divide show how easy it is to accept a theory which gives a stand-in for oneself a prominent place and with which one therefore can really identify. It is not difficult to recognize in the philosophical subject of knowledge the generalized Ego. The tenacity with which the subject–object theory of knowledge remained for hundreds of years a leading theory reminds one of the constancy with which a geocentric theory of the universe maintained its rule. It was pleasant to know that one's own habitat was the centre of the universe. Irrefutable evidence was at hand to confirm the erroneous hypothesis. The sun travelled day by day over the sky, apparently around the earth. Yet, the mistake was discovered.

In this case one can clearly distinguish between data which are symbolic representations and those which are not, and which for that reason are classified in a different manner: they are classified as real. Philosophy in the tradition of Descartes is above all a philosophy of doubt. It teaches its disciples to doubt. What those successors taught was not necessarily, and in many cases decidedly not, a way beyond the doubt, but the merits of doubt as such. The basic doubt was directed against the assumption that human beings may learn how the objects of their knowledge are structured quite independently of the fact that they are objects of human knowledge. Philosophers in the succession of Descartes, Kant, Husserl and Popper imputed to those they regarded as pre-Cartesian the view that one fine day humans will wake up to find that they know the objects of knowledge independently of the fact that they are objects of human knowledge. Philosophers at the Cartesian stage did not always explicitly postulate that knowledge falsifies. They merely said: it is possible; humans can never know whether that is the case or not; the honest thing to do is to say: we are in doubt.

An example may be of help. It is by now an old well-liked story how the Scottish philosopher David Hume noticed that individual people cannot possibly acquire through their own individual experience the concept of a causal connection as a universal type of explanation. And how he thus was the first to discover a fundamental philosophical problem: if not as a result of their own experience, how on earth do human beings come by the expectation that all unsolved problems can find a solution in the form of a cause-and-effect connection? David Hume was baffled and, being a modest person, he confessed that he knew no answer to the question.

The great Immanuel Kant continued the search for an answer to Hume's problem, and proudly announced in his *Critique of Pure Reason* that he had found it. He agreed with Hume that the expectation of a causal solution to an almost unlimited variety of problems could not possibly be derived from an individual's own experience. But he went beyond Hume by declaring that the universal human expectation of a cause-and-effect connection which might eventually be found as a solution of all outstanding problems, was a characteristic of human reason itself, like 'substance', 'god', and a number of other basic concepts. Kant's solution to the problem was simple and, if correct, far-reaching in its consequences. According to him the ubiquity of causal connections was not due to their factual recurrence in the world as such but to the structure of the human intellect. Causal connections, according to Kant, were built into human reason prior to any experience or, in other words, *a priori*. It did not transcend experience; if that were the case, causal connections could be regarded as fantasies and speculations. Kant regarded it as his great discovery that specific forms of reasoning, causal connections among them, were not transcendent to human experience but universal conditions of all human experiences or, in Kant's language, transcendental. He sharply distinguished between two concepts which before could be more or less used as identical. He decreed that from now on philosophers should distinguish unequivocally between the term 'transcendent', which might be derived from experience and yet transcend experience, and the term 'transcendental', which he saw as a presupposition of experience and which as such could be derived from a systematic observation of experiences.

Kant's transcendentalism had grave consequences. It implied that human beings can never know whether the world as such has all those characteristics which it appears to have when it passes through consciousness or reason. For in that case it acquires some of those properties which are predetermined by the nature of human reason, by characteristics of the human mind itself. According to Kant human reasoning was not capable of adapting itself to all possible types of experience. It was not infinitely variable in accordance with the manifoldness of the world itself. As a means of orientation human reasoning, according to Kant, had definite limits. We are compelled to fit our experiences into a predetermined pattern dictated by human nature. The compelling force of the expectation of finding solutions to all kinds of problems in the form of a cause-and-effect connection can serve as example. It does not originate from the nature of the objects of reasoning, but from the nature of the subjects. Unintentionally Kant was a promoter of philosophical relativism.

And yet, it is not particularly difficult to move towards a

solution the problem raised by Hume, which Kant believed he had solved. The belief in the satisfying nature of causal solutions of problems of all kinds cannot be founded on the experience of individual people. Is it based on the nature of human reasoning? What other solutions offer themselves? The most immediate answer is simple enough. There is no need for a place of refuge in the assumption of a naturally predetermined form of reasoning. The term 'cause' and its various uses are acquired through a process of learning by all normally endowed members of a contemporary language community. Why did this obvious answer escape Hume and Kant? Probably because it was not the answer to *their* problem, to the problem as it presented itself to people brought up in the philosophical tradition. They expected a causal answer, attuned to their individualistic tradition. It was this tradition which found expression in Hume's layout of the question, as in Kant's answer. Not acquired through individual experience, which is far too limited for a judgment of this scope, said Hume. Founded in the nature of human reasoning, replied Kant, using a causal model. Social explanations, the knowledge that acquisition of a language and thus of words such as 'cause' and 'effect' is something more than an accumulation of individual actions, was beyond the reach of both. Nor were they ready to recognize the social contentment attached to the finding of a causal explanation as an aspect of the social habitus of a period, as a form of social compulsion.

The expectation of a specific type of explanation is not due to an individual's personal experience, but to the collective experiences of a whole group in the course of many generations. If they grow up in a society where witchcraft has undoubtedly come to be regarded as the most powerful force, individuals are likely to find the socially required answer to their urgent questions when they find the witch who has caused the damage they try to explain. Both Hume and Kant had learned the quest for causal explanation and the term 'cause' itself from childhood on as a self-evident ingredient of their language. One may well ask why this obvious answer escaped their grip. The reason presumably was that in their society and in their profession solutions of this type, social solutions, had not the cognitive value and were not accompanied by the same feeling of satisfaction by which they might be accompanied today. In point of fact, the assumption that the search for impersonal causes is the favourite search for ex-

planation at all periods of time is hardly correct. It was generally
preceded, and often accompanied, by the search for living persons
as authors of happenings, and by the conception of all happenings
as actions one tried to explain. The question 'Who has destroyed
my house by lightning?' preceded the question 'What has destroyed my house?' In the development of humanity, causal
explanations gained a partial supremacy rather late. Most living
people probably still seek an answer to the question 'Who has
created the world?' not 'What changes account for the present
constellation of the physical universe?' The search for long-term
process-explanations is still in an early phase.

People can experience the world now as nature or now as
history. One can see the world in the manner of Newton as design
produced by a great spirit: all that happens is subject to a perfect
order. Seen as nature the events of this world repeat themselves
again and again. It obediently follows immutable laws which the
great designer has prescribed for it. Its reward is the great
harmony in which all beings live with each other. The majestic rise
of the morning sun above the horizon, the grandeur of the
declining evening sun bear witness to the realism of this conception of the world as nature eternally following its prescribed
course.

But one can also see this world as history. In this case too it has
its regularities. If one chooses this approach the sun becomes
recognizable as a medium-sized star like millions of others. The
beauty of the luminous sky of a cloudless summer need not conceal
its indifference to the human fate. After a foreseeable number of
years the life-sustaining atomic reactions of the sun will lose these
faculties. It is likely to disintegrate through a sequence of phases
well known from the observation of other stars of this kind. The
coming and going of our sun system is as unique as the Battle of
Waterloo within the nameless universe of which it forms part.
And, indeed, the Battle of Waterloo forms part of the same
universe to which in whatever form my writing desk belongs. After
a while the conditions which gave rise to the type of self-regulating
organization we call life are likely to disappear.

From the fact that humans can experience the world in two
different ways, in a world which can be represented most clearly
by means of symbols of unchanging regularities and a world
representing the structure of a ceaseless sequential change in one
or two complementary directions, one may easily come to the

conclusion that this world consists of two different universes, one of which is characterized by the code-word 'nature', the other by that of 'history' or 'culture'. In fact these code-words represent two different modes of ordering experiences. For reasons which are not immediately obvious our world admits of two different ways of selecting and ordering perceptions. It is not unlikely that in some cases the one, in other cases the other may be more reality-adequate, or that different problem fields require different blendings of these two types of symbolic representation.

Human beings, who represent what is probably one of the rarest events within nature, may have time and perhaps even opportunities for making their life with each other more pleasant, more comfortable and meaningful than it has been so far. No one can do that for human beings; they must do that themselves. It is unlikely that they will find in the few million years left to them anything better to do than to search for just that, for the production of better conditions of life on earth for themselves and for all those they have chosen as companions on this way. Of course, it is possible that humans are threatened by dangers as yet unknown, by dangers associated with pain, and which are likely to curtail the joy of life, which have been curtailed so far and which may be further curtailed by humans themselves. In that case more or perhaps all human beings may take it upon themselves to decide that death is preferable to any further life on earth. In accordance with the responsibility given to them as the only creatures capable of informed and planned cooperation — the only beings capable of such action — they may decide that the future is likely to steer humanity into a position where the chances of suffering would outweigh the chances of joy. If not all, many human beings may decide in such a situation that it is reasonable to end the conditions which made life possible on earth or wherever humanity's offspring may have settled by then. It may be advisable in such a situation to leave the decision about the life and death of humanity to the individuals concerned. I am mentioning this possibility merely in order to make it quite clear that the continued concealment of the true conditions under which human beings may find it worth while to continue their common life wherever it is possible, and know exactly, as far as that is humanly possible, what is in store for them.

One may perhaps feel that the use of the terms 'language', 'knowledge', 'memory' and others belonging to the same knowledge complex deviates from their customary usage. According to a widespread custom different functions of this knowledge complex are usually understood as if the different linguistic expressions used in any particular language as representative sound patterns for the various functions of this knowledge complex referred to different separately existing objects. Thus, the language function of a knowledge process may be socially treated as one object, the knowledge function as another, the memory function as a third. This tendency to treat different functions of the same knowledge complex as if they were separately and independently existing objects has been abandoned in this text. There different functions of one and the same knowledge process are not treated as if they were substantially different. Instead they are treated as what they are, as different functions of a substantially identical knowledge complex. The same can be said of the characteristics as properties of individuals and societies. Languages, thoughts, memories and all the other aspects of knowledge complexes are not treated here as either individual or social. They are always perceived as potentially and actually both, social and individual at the same time.

Other distinctions undergo analogous corrections. Thus one can observe the tendency to treat familiar distinctions as if they had been known to people from time immemorial. The distinction between living and non-living objects is a graphic example. Thus, one may be inclined to assume that people in all ages knew the difference between living and non-living things in the same way it is known today. However, it is well enough known that this distinction, once upon a time, was less realistic and less sharp than it is today. One of the characteristics of the mode of thinking we call mythical is the attribution of properties of the living to objects we now know to be inanimate. It is after all only in this century that humans have begun to have a reasonably realistic knowledge of the events which enable the sun to give light and warmth tirelessly to the inhabitants of the earth. Not knowing the nature of molecular fusion made it easier for people to attribute to the happenings at the level of the sun the character of actions at the human level. It is not particularly daring to guess at the overall direction of the process of growth of humanity's knowledge. In order to reach its present condition humanity's reality-congruent knowledge must have become more extensive for thousands of years.

Given the present field of observation it may seem daring to speak of humanity as the social unit of knowledge growth, yet there are weighty reasons which make it advisable to treat the growth of humankind as the matrix of the growth of knowledge. In the long run it is difficult and perhaps impossible for any particular sub-group of humanity to appropriate particular advances in knowledge. In the competitive struggles of human groups advances in knowledge often play a decisive part. Moreover, it is easier to steal knowledge which gives advantage to a group than almost any other advantageous property of people.

A specific linguistic form, called a question, often serves as point of departure on the road towards new knowledge. It is also one of the distinguishing marks of human beings. They are the only animate beings capable of asking questions. Questions indicate the limits of a person's or a group's fund of knowledge. They are directed from someone who does not know at someone or something which is expected to know the answer. Today, at a period of knowledge growth when one is able to distinguish more or less realistically between human subjects and non-living objects, questions can be directed from a living subject at a non-living object. Once upon a time they could be directed only from one member of a human or a spirit world at another. One must make allowance too for a different meaning of terms such as 'subject' and 'object' or their equivalents in a society where nature was experienced more as the playground of spirits than as that of atoms and molecules.

The term 'object', in the context of an object–subject antithesis, still retains a fairly close association not with objects in general but with lifeless objects, with objects of the physical sciences. Nor has it ceased to be the exponent of a tradition of long standing which enjoins its adherents to perceive differences as opposites, eternally engaged in a warfare with each other, such as nature and culture, objects not made by people and objects made by people. As used today, 'nature' is in fact a conglomerate of often divergent evaluations. The use of the word 'nature' or of one of its affiliates can be value-lowering, for instance if it is used in connection with 'matter', and thus with materialism, and value-enhancing if it is used in opposition to that which is human-made. It can have undertones of materialism and undertones of idealism. In its traditional form the human problem of cognition does not admit an enduring answer, an answer which can command the consensus of its explorers. It can be used as representative of the entire universe and then again as representative of the non-human layers of the universe only and as antipode to the human or cultural layers.

Since Descartes first raised the basic cognitive question not very much has changed. The same question has been asked throughout the centuries. In a very simplified form the question which demanded an answer was: How can a person ever be sure that the answer to a question that has been found is the correct answer, or — in classical language — that the answer is true? Scientific knowledge advanced by leaps and bounds. The doubt as to the certainty of scientific answers, as to their correspondence to any really existing world, stubbornly retained its full strength. In course of time a variety of answers to this question have been given by learned men from Descartes via Kant to Husserl and Popper. Whatever the answer was, the Cartesian doubt raised its head throughout the centuries we call modern times with un-diminished force. The diagnosis changed but the illness remained the same. Throughout modern times humanity's store of reality-oriented knowledge steadily grew. But the doubts as to the nature of this knowledge did not disappear. Whether a 'real world' corresponded to the changing scientific symbols of it remained uncertain. One would have to take a considerable risk if one were to say that since the days of Descartes and Kant not only has knowledge itself grown but also the certainty that the real world corresponds to the extended scientific knowledge of it. One could find a good deal of evidence for the opposite view, for the view that scientific knowledge of nature and society has grown by leaps and bounds but the conviction that the world really is as the symbols of sciences show it to be has hardly increased among learned people. There is a good deal of evidence for the view that the belief in the reality-congruence of scientific knowledge has decreased rather than increased. Among learned people one tends to avoid expressions such as 'reality' or 'realism' in the context of a discussion about human knowledge. Otherwise one is suspected of not having learned the great lesson to be learned from classical European philosophy, the recognition that knowledge is not simply a mirror image or a replica of that which is known. In fact, one might say that characteristic of the post-Cartesian period is the simultaneity of an accelerating process of knowledge growth and of a steady, perhaps even a growing uncertainty about the relationship between knowledge and that which it claims to represent, the unknown world. An unparalleled expansion of knowledge which presents itself as realistic with a built-in animus against fantasy knowledge goes hand in hand with a continuous doubt as to the existence of anything independently of the knower. That is the worm in the apple of modernity.

Societies such as ours with firmly established scientific institutions and professions as a rule routinely produce more new knowledge than societies at a pre-scientific stage of development. They also often enough produce a nagging doubt as to the mode of existence of objects of knowledge independently of oneself. They are vivid examples of the fact that new knowledge is not only produced in individual isolation but also in accordance with the stage of development characteristic of a society at a given time. The prevailing theories of knowledge use as their model a condition in which knowledge might be produced by an individual alone. They pay little attention to the problems one encounters if the social conditions of knowledge production are taken into account. If that is done, epistemological questions of the Cartesian or Kantian type lose much of their cognitive value. Questions such as that of the use and meaning of causal terms in society at large move into the centre of the problem field. Kant (like other people) learned the concept of an explanation in general, and, in particular, explanations in the purely secular, wholly impersonal form of a cause-and-effect connection, as part of his mother tongue. Like other concepts, that of a cause-and-effect connection could only be acquired as part of the social usages of one's society. Hume's observation that the concept of a causal connection could not be explained in terms of the personal experiences of a single individual, was entirely correct. It represents a level of conceptual synthesis which is beyond the reach of the personal experiences of a human individual. It presupposes a capacity for connecting events at a level which no individual person can attain unaided by the experiences of other persons. It presupposes a biological constitution of a species which makes it possible for its individual representatives to learn, to store and to act upon experiences made and transmitted to that person by a long line of antecedent generations.

We are entirely ignorant of the conditions under which a species of living beings emerged from an evolutionary process, equipped not only for learning from their elders, but also for storing and for, potentially, turning to their advantage ancestral experiences made and transmitted in course of time through a continuous sequence of generations. The mode of intergenerational transmission of experiences itself is no mystery. Ancestral experiences can be deposited in the concepts of a language, and can thus be handed on through a line of generations of considerable length. The sequential order of generational experiences itself can have considerable significance for the pattern of experience transmitted from generation to generation. Deposits of earlier experiences can be reinforced, blocked and, for all we know, perhaps even extinguished by those of later generations. For the time being it may be enough to draw attention to the incompleteness of the prevailing techniques of connecting patterns of group fortunes and group characteristics.

The difficulty which one encounters here is in no small measure due to the fact that the changing characteristics of individual members of the group are related but by no means identical with the changing characteristics of the group. Rome between AD 200 and 300 changed. So did the Romans during the same period. But the two types of changes so closely related require different expressions. To bear fruit a process-sociological approach to language and knowledge has to distance itself from the approach which has come to be known as historical. The latter is pre-eminently concerned with short-term sociological processes. In historical terms a century may be a long-time distance; in process-sociological terms it can become recognizable as a time span of short duration. Historians often are only able to use the life-span of an individual as yardstick for changes at other social levels, e.g. changes of the spoken language or of priestly knowledge. And in that case many connections of an ongoing knowledge process may remain unnoticed and invisible.

The skills required for the study of long-term processes may still need some time to mature. Specific hurdles have to be overcome before social processes of long duration can become a regular study object.

(UNFINISHED)

I

In human communications words represent objects of all kinds, including functions and imaginations. How these words come to represent these objects is an open problem. More attention to it might be rewarding. Why does 'étoile' represent for French people what 'star' represents for English people? There seems to be a barrier which blocks a widely acceptable answer to questions of this kind. I will give two preliminary clues which may help to clarify the nature of this impediment. Both are simple. They can appear obvious. Yet their relevance to the problem of language communication can be easily overlooked.

The first clue is the easily testable, one may perhaps say the trivial, observation that visitors to a country where one speaks a language they do not know cannot communicate with them by means of a language unless they have a third language in common. Given the fact that communication by means of a language is the principal form of communication between humans, it is a remarkable characteristic of humanity that there are so many different languages on earth. There is a single humanity, the only species using a language as its principal means of communication; there are and were hundreds, perhaps altogether thousands, of different languages preventing communication between different groups. Almost all self-ruling and quite a number of no longer self-ruling groups have a language of their own. Maybe that once upon a time, at the very early stage of humanity's development, only one human group existed on earth speaking rudiments of the same language. Perhaps, at some future date, all human beings besides their own local or regional language may have one language in common. But all these are speculation. Nevertheless they are not entirely useless. They make us aware that language as it is unites and disunites, integrates and disintegrates. The dual function is significant. More shall be heard about it later.

Human beings are members of a unified species and at the same time members of different societies. This duplex character of humans is apt to give rise to misjudgement and misunderstanding. What is biological and common to all human beings is judged to be social; what is social is judged to be biological. I have already referred to the fact that the same objects were represented in different societies by different words. It is difficult to think of any other species whose principal form of communication was capable of an equally high degree of social differentiation.

One can hardly come to grips with the problem mentioned before, that of the relationship between words and events, without paying attention to the fact that human societies with different languages may equip their members with different words for similar objects. It is obvious that the potential for communicating by means of a language is part of the unlearned biological heritage of humanity. It is equally obvious that this natural potential for language communication of the human species becomes operative only if it is activated by a social process of individual learning. The learning-pattern of languages can differ greatly from society to society. Many languages spoken by humans have disappeared. Others developed continuously and survived to this day. That too is fairly obvious. Language theory may perhaps neglect the fact that the propensity for language communication is a common characteristic of the whole species and any specific language only of a particular society, of a limited section of the species. One need only think of the many attempts made in the past to teach apes the rudiments of one of the human languages. They were doomed from the outset. Apes have local variations of their unlearned species-specific means of communication, but it is far less malleable through varieties of social learning than the human language potential. The tower of Babel experience, the extent to which languages integrate societies but divide the species, is uniquely human.

If facts which are fairly obvious and easy to observe are frequently neglected in the work of scientists, one can be fairly sure the neglect has a reason. It is usually a sign of a characteristic flaw in their work. More often than not, the blockages are due to an intellectual defect frequently found among academics. One might call it *academismus*. Its main feature is the projection of academic departmentalization and the rivalries connected with it into the subject matter of departmental research. And thus biologists and, indeed, all those scientific specialists who are proud to work with the classical models of natural sciences, tend to theorize about language rather than languages. In point of fact, the animal kingdom offers no other examples of a species' means of communication which are malleable and subject to social differentiation to the same extent as the human capacity for language communication. Biologists, however, seek as a matter of course to maintain their dominion over the human problem field by selecting for attention all those characteristics of humans which they have in common with other species and obscure or deny all structural characteristics of humans which are unique, which distinguish the human species from pre-human species. The multiplicity of languages and all other aspects of languages which are specific to society rather than to species, do not fit the biologists' departmental goal.

On the one hand, the sociologists' attitude in this matter indicates a certain confusion. They have not yet clearly emancipated themselves from the models of the natural sciences. Hence for them, too, law-like universals such as language have a higher cognitive status than a multitude of different human languages for which hardly a precedent can be found in the non-human realm. On the other hand, sociologists appear to be very determined to protect their own autonomy and independence. Explicitly or not they tend to reject the biologists' claim that the study of humans, and thus of human societies, is a subdivision of biology. The result is another blockage of observation and reflection. The relationship between biological evolution and social development as a topic of research is almost wholly excluded from the sociologists' field of teaching and research. Altogether, biologists and sociologists proceed as if the biological and the social aspects of human beings were as strictly divided from, and independent of, each other as the two professions of biologists and sociologists and, in any specific case, as the two departments of biology and sociology wish to be. Consequently, neither of the two professions can come to grips with a fact which is of some importance for the understanding of the symbol theory, introduced in the following pages. This is the fact that, in reality, biological and social processes depend on each other; they dovetail into each other when human beings first learn to speak a language. Far from being as independent as the respective academic professions and departments want it to be, the biological disposition for learning a language which matures in the early days of every human being, is by nature dependent on social activation, on the stimulating contact with older persons speaking a specific language, the language of a specific society.

The second clue throws light on one of the basic difficulties of the social sciences at the present stage of their development. As in the case of the first clue, the core of the difficulty can be traced back to a blockage of knowledge. But in this case it is not present type of academic specialization which causes the trouble, but the prototypical way in which people experience themselves in the more developed societies of our age and in the way this self-image finds expression in the theories of social sciences. The self-image to which I refer is that of oneself and, generally, of all human beings as essentially independent actors. Twentieth-century sociology offers some well-known examples of this self-image. Weber's and Parsons's action theories are among the best known of these examples. In the form of a theory of communicative action they have been extended by Habermas with special regard to the problem of human communication. But it would be a mistake to attribute the blockage of knowledge which one can observe in all these theories, only or mainly to the authors of these theories. They are spokespersons and representative of a distinctive social habitus which is characteristic of our age. It induces in people the feeling that in some sense their individual self and, by proxy, every other individual, exists as a kind of monad independently of all others in a central position in the world and that one can explain all social events, including human communication, in terms of individual actions. In this case, too, a strong desire to be independent and autonomous leads to an intellectual black-out of the fact that the message of one person can only be understood by another if it is couched in terms of a common code. In the human case a language is that code. The monadic action model of communication is apt to block understanding of this fact. It is significant that, as Leibniz saw it, monads have no windows and cannot communicate directly, only via God. The nature of language cannot be understood if one uses individual actions as a point of departure.

But in this case the blockage goes deeper than it does if one forgets that languages not only make possible but also limit communication. It goes to the root of the present forms of thinking, of period-specific categories used as if they were universals. The prevailing codes direct us to search for beginnings. Most languages used today have no recognizable beginning and it is difficult to imagine such a beginning. By no stretch of the imagination can one regard a language as a composite unit formed by a number of individual actions as its constituent elements. A language, in order to serve its function as means of communication, must be known and used by a plurality of people at the same time. An individual action involving the use of language would be pointless if no one but a single actor knew that language. In that respect language can serve as the prototypical model of a social fact. It presupposes the existence not only of *one* actor, but of a group of two or more co-acting people. It fosters and at the same time requires a degree of group integration. In any given case a group of language speakers exists prior to the individual speaking act. A language, in other words, cannot be dissolved into individual actions, communicative or otherwise. It is as it were the prototype of a beginningless process.

Relevant facts are obvious and well known. Yet some basic aspects of languages, their implications and the conclusions to be drawn from them, are rarely explored. Here, too, one encounters a characteristic blockage of knowledge. The obvious fact is that every human being normally learns in early childhood a language which has been spoken by others before that individual child was born. The very obviousness of this fact may disguise the apparent paradox and the temptation to metaphysics which one encounters here. To put it at its simplest, an intense desire of individual human beings to recognize themselves as existing in complete independence as wholly autonomous human beings may militate against the recognition that the language one speaks, which forms an integral part of one's personality, is a social fact presupposing the existence of other human beings and preceding the existence of any particular individual. If every human being, in order to become fully human, has to learn a pre-existing language, does one not have to conclude that language has an extra-human existence, that it exists in some sense independently of all human beings? That a given language has a degree of independence and autonomy in relation to any particular individual, is easy to observe. If an English-speaking person uses the English language arbitrarily, the communicative function of language is impaired and may eventually lapse. The compelling force which a language has in relation to its individual users is not the result of an extra-human, quasi-metaphysical existence of language, but of the fact that language loses its function and indeed its character as a language if it is understood by one speaker alone. To be operative as language the sound patterns of a language have to be understood by other human beings as well as by a given individual speaker. The compelling force of a language has its root in the fact that it represents a unified canon of speaking which has to be observed by a whole group of people if it is to maintain its communicative function.

But there is more to it. The statement that every human being, if it is to become fully human, has to learn in early childhood a pre-existing language from his or her elders, given the traditional customs of thinking, seems to invite the question: where did it all begin? Shall one speculatively assume that at some unknown stage in the past human beings started the language tradition which manifests itself today in the contemporary English language? Shall one perhaps even assume that at some unknown date human beings started to use a language as their medium of communication instead of some unknown pre-human, pre-verbal form of communication?

These questions vividly represent one of the characteristic imperatives of the ruling convention of speaking and thinking. The convention finds expression in a powerful intellectual need to discover absolute beginnings. In this context, too, one discovers behind the disguises, which may be highly sophisticated and often obscure, questions concerning priorities of the start or the origin. Does one have to begin from social data in order to understand individuals? Does one have to start from individual actions in order to understand social data such as languages? The answer is simple. But it runs counter to some deep-rooted conventions of knowledge and thought with a firm anchorage in the traditional languages. Many aspects of the real world, which is the object of scientific explorations, have the character of a process often with recognizable transitions to a new stage, but without any absolute beginning. Whatever one may say about the Big Bang, which is sometimes considered as an absolute start from nowhere, our universe as a whole forms part of a beginningless process. References to an absolute beginning may seem to give a safe anchorage to the human need for orientation. But the safety they provide is treacherous. One secures peace of mind for oneself by stopping to ask questions. Who created the world? A creator. Uncertainty seems to be conquered because one stops asking questions. One does not ask: who created the creator? The same applies to the English language. It applies to the whole world. One gains a false security for one's sense of orientation by not asking for the Why of the Why, for the causes of causes.

The statement that all human beings have to learn in early childhood a pre-existing language may seem to confront the receiver of the message with an unsolvable puzzle. How can a language come into being without human beings? But it presents a puzzle that is difficult to solve only if one feels compelled by the pressure of one's social habitus and tradition to ask for absolute beginnings. If human beings could look at themselves with a higher degree of detachment, they could easily recognize that two processes very different in their dynamics and structure play a part in their making. As it is, they are not very clearly distinguished and often not at all. They are commonly known by names such as 'evolution' or 'development'. But their relationship and their differences are seldom set out clearly. A slightly contemptuous word, the term 'evolutionism' is often used indiscriminately for both and little attention is paid to the fact that, distinct as they are, evolution made development possible. Both processes are centred on the transmission of means of survival from generation to generation and with their changes, some of which help to improve these chances. But what is transmitted and how it is transmitted differs greatly in the two cases. In the case of evolution, the chief instrument of transmission and change is an organic structure called the 'gene'. In the case of development, the chief instrument of transmission and change are symbols in the wide sense of the word including not only knowledge, but, for example, also standards of conduct and sentiment. Initially, language transmission from person to person was its principal form.

It has been usual to use terms such as 'evolution' and 'development' as almost identical or interchangeable. The difference was apparently not clear. A possible way to make the distinction quite clear is the limitation of the term 'evolution' as symbol of the biological process achieved through gene-transmission and to confine the term 'development' to intergenerational symbol transmission in all its various forms. Both types of processes have the character of a sequence in which later, more differentiated and integrated objects of transmission follow earlier objects of transmission. Languages are an example, perhaps the most telling and original of all. For the sounds which pre-human animals use as means of communication, mostly together with other bodily gestures and postures, lack the representation function which give human-made sounds the character of a language. They lack the property which gives many, though by no means all, human-made sounds the character of symbols and thus of a language. Like groans, sighs and the cries of extreme pain, pre-language sounds are gene-transmitted signals which indicate the condition of the makers of these sounds to their fellows. They are, in a word, species-specific, not group-specific. The sounds which form the main means of communication of human beings, the various languages, on the other hand, are not species-specific but group-specific.

If human questioners can tone down their involvement and adjust their questions to the realities of their world, one finds oneself confronted with an articulated process without beginning leading, for example, from ancestral groups with dominant pre-verbal forms of communication, without any absolute break to the emergence of ancestors with dominant verbal communication. Most details escape us at the present stage of knowledge, but it is fairly safe to assume that in this case, as in so many others, an evolutionary process with many intermediary steps in course of time reached a condition of optimal functionality. Languages share with some other properties of humans one of the unique distinctions of the human species. They can change without changes in the human gene structure, and thus potentially also improve — characteristics which in all other known species are hardened in a genetically determined form. Alterations of their language, for example, can occur solely in conjunction with a group's fortunes, without changes in their belongingness to the human species. People of the same descent who form, or belong to, different groups, may find that in some respects the ancestral language in different groups has developed in different ways. The reason is obvious. Unlike pre-human types of sound communication whose dominant form is genetically determined and not acquired through learning, languages as a means of communication have to be acquired through learning. Human beings, by their biological constitution, are prepared for the acquisition of a language through individual learning at an early age. But they are not by nature equipped with a language. They are by nature only equipped with the disposition for learning a language from elders who care for them. This is an example of the interlocking between natural maturation, and thus in the last resort between biological evolution on the one hand and social development on the other.

Human nature offers a disposition for language learning which remains dormant if the social conditions for its evocation are absent. By nature, in other words, humans are not only equipped with the possibility, but also with the need for acquiring from others through learning a language as their principal means of communication. The dominant customs of knowledge and thought may make it appear that conceptual distinction and division, such as that between the processes of biological evolution and social development, is identical with a simple factual independence and juxtaposition of the processes concerned. It may be thus at first a bit difficult to understand that, in the case of humans, the limited autonomy of their social development in relation to human nature goes hand in hand with a specific interdependence. The natural potential of young humans can only unfold itself through appropriate contact with other humans. In certain respects, human nature and human society, far from being antipodes, intertwine and thus depend on each other. The human capability for changing in the manner of a social development and without any biological changes is itself based on the biological constitution of human beings. The biological evolution which made it possible and necessary for human beings to acquire their principal means of communicating with their fellows through individual learning, also made it possible that these means of communication can change without biological changes or, in other words, can develop.

In present scientific discussions the terms 'nature' and 'society' are sometimes used as if these two fields of research were exclusive antagonists. The implied assumption seems to be that objects or conditions which belong to the field of nature cannot belong to the field of society and vice versa. But the representation of these two fields as antagonists is more characteristic of the present relationship between the groups of scientific specialists devoted to the research in these different fields than of the factual relationship between these two fields itself. The fact, mentioned before, that biologists and sociologists sometimes act as if they were guardians of national territories separated by clear-cut boundaries, thrusts both into the role of competitors at loggerheads with regard to their ill-defined boundaries. If it is genetically determined, it is generally understood to belong to the realm of biology. If it is acquired by experience or, in other words, by learning, it is widely understood not to be a biological problem. But the relationship between prehuman species and the human species has the character of a process. It is a pure fiction to expect one day clear-cut boundaries to emerge between the biological and the human sciences, comparable to national boundaries. This leaves the whole field intermediary between possibly ancestral more ape-like species and the human species, even as a field of hypothesis, unexplored and thus also the possibility to improve the understanding of the distinctiveness of the human development.

Apart from three or four species of apes, no members of this descent line, except human beings, have survived the struggle for survival. The apes are surviving the struggle rather precariously while human beings come out more and more clearly as the dominant species on earth. But the properties which account for their position within the ongoing struggle are still far from clear. They are concealed rather than revealed by commonsense words such as 'intellect' or 'mind'. They are concealed, too, by the disappearance from the living of all the representatives of intermediary stages between non-human species and the human species. The coincidences of the struggle which have allowed only humans and a few species of apes to survive, have created a rather foreshortened picture of the human descent. It has created the impression that the immediate, more animalic forebears of human beings looked and behaved like apes. It has induced attempts at teaching young apes one of the human languages with complete disregard for the fact that communication by means of sets of socially standardized symbols represents a novel technique of communication compared with the largely genetically fixated sounds which serve apes as one of their means of communication. At present we have no idea of the intermediary evolutionary steps leading from the largely innate and species-specific sounds which form part of the known communication equipment of animals to the biological equipment which makes it possible to acquire with the help of a personal learning process the representational equipment of a language. The disappearance from the living species of all representatives of intermediary stages between the usually more species-specific sounds which help other species to communicate and the human form of representational and socially standardized communication, makes it difficult even to guess how the novel technique of communication came into being. This is certainly not the only novel technique which gave humans their strong position in the struggle for survival. What it suggests is that the usual picture of a relatively short descent line leading from ape-like creatures to humans is misleading. The immense human capacity for storing in memory and for recalling from there, if required, personal experiences, which is one of the conditions for learning to use a language, in all likelihood required for its evolution a much longer and much more complicated line of descent than that represented by what is by now almost a commonsense picture of the descent of humans from beings which resembled the living species of apes.

The disappearance of intermediaries is most certainly not confined to the human ancestry. It is a common characteristic of animal descent. The descent line of horses, whose contemporary hoofed representatives were preceded by four-legged animals equipped with toed feet, is a well-known example of the disappearance of intermediaries. The organisms equipped in this manner functioned better than those representing intermediary steps. At this optimal stage this particular process stopped. Representatives of the intermediary stages with a lesser survival value than those of the optimal stage disappeared after a longer or shorter struggle for survival. To a later observer, therefore, the representatives of a pre-optimal but continuous evolutionary process can easily appear as representatives of a sudden jump and perhaps as an absolute beginning. But this impression is simply created by the fact that in many, though not necessarily in all cases, the representatives of pre-optimal stages on the road to optimal functionality are likely to die out once an evolutionary process within its niche, which may be smaller or larger, has reached its optimal form. Disappearance of the intermediaries, in all likelihood, is a frequently occurring aspect of evolutionary processes. In this context the concept of optimal functionality may help to draw attention to the fact that what needs attention is not only the fact that evolutionary processes occur under certain conditions, but also to the fact that such processes can go on for a while in a specific direction and then cease to go on beyond a certain stage. Language communication in the form in which we know it was presumably one aspect of a long and continuous evolutionary process which stopped when it reached an optimal form. What did not stop was the development of languages. The capacity for learning and speaking a language is a common property of all normal members of the human species. It has long been accepted that the changes which human societies and human beings as their part can undergo are of two distinctly different types.

Whether the evolutionary process of the human species and, more particularly, of its language propensity continues or has come to a halt, is not a question which needs to be discussed here. What deserves attention is the distinction between the biological process of evolution and the development of any particular language. The latter is not a biological process. It is not a species-specific but a group-specific change of language, which can occur while all the

biological characteristics of the human beings concerned remain
unchanged. Our present languages are not richly enough endowed
to do justice to the ramification and manifoldedness of observable
natural and social processes. The development of languages can
itself serve as example. From a certain phase on, it is a development,
a non-evolutionary process made possible by an evolutionary
innovation perhaps after a long process evolutionary and developmental in character at the same time. The human vocal apparatus
can illustrate this complexity. It is part of a biological evolution
which gave rise to a new non-evolutionary type of process — a
language development. At the present stage many language changes
are purely social and not genetic or evolutionary in character. But
one can imagine an earlier stage in which biological and social
aspects of hominid evolution went hand in hand.

The growth process of a child may still show residual traces of this
long phase in the continuous evolutionary process during which the
novel technique of communicating by means of a learned language
gained the upper hand over the communication largely by inborn
signals. Just as the transformation of a tadpole evolving into a frog
may still contain residues of the continuous transformation of water
animals into land animals, so the transformation of a still largely
animalic human baby, communicating by means of inborn non-
verbal signals, into an emerging human being ready to learn communicating by means of a language, is a continuous process perhaps
with residues of the evolutionary humanization of animals.

An evolutionary change is sometimes represented as a straight line
process. That may be, but is not always, the case. A continuous
evolutionary process can result in the emergence of an entirely new
biological structure and in a new manner of living, as in the cases of
sea animals evolving into land animals, of reptiles into birds. The
distinction introduced here between biological evolution and social
development is another example. The developmental character of
changes is not confined to languages. Everything social is subject to
developmental types of changes. But at present the two types of
processes, the evolutionary and the developmental, are conceptually
not clearly distinguished. One may speak of a breakthrough to a new
structure, but the apparent suddenness and discontinuity of the
emergence of evolutionary innovations may be simply due, as has
been mentioned before, to the disappearance of intermediary stages
after the emergence of a better functioning organism as competitor
in the same setting. It is possible that the transition from more

ape-like ancestors to human beings was a process of this kind. The disappearance of the intermediaries may easily conceal the extent of the biological innovation represented by humans if they are in their own imagination compared with more ape-like ancestors.

One of the most striking innovatory characteristics which distinguishes humans from apes is the fact that, in the case of ape societies and ape communications, genetically determined forms still predominate over local variations acquired through learning. In the case of humans the latter have gained unequivocally the upper hand over the former. Human societies and human languages can change to an extent inaccessible to the societies and the means of communication of apes. The structure of the latter is still largely genetically fixated or, in other words, species-specific. In the case of human societies and human languages the malleability, the ability to change, has become so great that extensive changes of social life, and thus also of languages, can occur within the biological lifetime of the same species. Human societies, as well as human languages, can undergo processes still largely blocked in the case of apes. It would be useful if one could agree on different terms for the type of processes from which humans have emerged as a species just like the various species of apes and for the processes which human societies alone can undergo, which are non-evolutionary in character and which occur within one and the same species. My suggestion is, to repeat, to reserve the term 'evolution' for processes of the first type, for biological processes dependent on gene structure and to reserve the term 'development' for processes of a non-evolutionary kind which only groups of human beings can undergo, but not groups of apes. It was an evolutionary breakthrough process resulting not only in the improvement of the same biological technique, but in the emergence of entirely new structures. That of air-breathing land animals equipped with lungs emerging from water-breathing sea animals equipped with gills, is an example. The transformation of ape-like creatures communicating by means of largely species-specific signals into human beings communicating mainly by means of group-specific learned languages, is another. The breakthrough process may have taken many thousands, probably millions of years. As in other cases, representatives of intermediary stages have largely disappeared. At any given stage the emergence of a biological equipment with a higher survival value probably led to the extinction of related species which lacked this equipment.

Nor did the evolution of biological structures needed for the learning of verbal communication totally destroy the means of pre-verbal communication. Instances of the latter, such as smiling, groaning or crying in pain, still have a vivid function in human relations of communication. But it is an auxiliary function. These more spontaneous signals have in some cases, as in that of smiling, also come under a person's deliberate control. They may be descendants of an entirely automatic reaction pattern which has become partly controllable with deliberation. By and large, however, the remaining pre-verbal reaction patterns of human beings play their part as supporters of the principal human form of communication by means of verbal symbols which are group-specific not species-specific and can only be acquired through learning.

The difficulty one may have in comprehending the emergence of entirely novel structures from within a continuous process is to some extent due to the fact that our present mode of thinking, the structure of our categories, is attuned to relatively short time distances. The relatively short time-span of a human life appears to serve people as their principal frame of reference. Time distances of many thousands, many millions of years may surpass people's imagination. Yet time distances of that order form the indispensable frame of reference of many evolutionary changes. The compatibility of structural innovation and processual continuity remains incomprehensible as long as the structural changes are not firmly embedded into time distances of this larger order. Nor is the reminder of this kind of time distance an idle speculation without relevance for human beings. Without reference to this kind of time distance humans can hardly understand themselves. Without it their self-image is likely to remain arrested in the battle between advocates of two equally misleading alternatives.

One of them, favoured by biologists, is the view that humans are animals like all other animalic creatures. It justifies the easy transfer to humans of conclusions drawn from animal experiments and legitimizes biology as the basic human science. It implies an evolutionary process in a straight line, perhaps in a line of steady advance. The second alternative postulates, explicitly or not, an ontological discontinuity of the evolutionary process. Its advocates may or may not accept the theory of evolution and the evidence supporting it. Whichever it is, they speak and think in a manner that suggests a dual world split into two modes of existence such as body and mind. According to this view humans have originated partly or wholly in complete independence of the evolutionary process. This conception implies, in other words, an absolute discontinuity between animals and some aspects of humans, such as soul or reason. Without reference to the time-scale required for evolutionary changes it is difficult to understand that human beings emerged from animal ancestors in the course of a continuous process and yet are in certain respects unique and unlike any other animal on earth. Moreover, their unique properties emerge from, and are fully integrated into, their animal heritage.

Communication by means of one of many languages is one of these unique human properties. Compared with the dominant form of communication of other species, the biological potential for learning a language which humans possess is rather malleable. The manifoldness of human languages bears witness to it. The fluidity of human languages contrasts sharply with the comparative rigidity of all animal forms of communication which are generally the same for a whole species with relatively small group-specific variations. There are other examples of human uniqueness. The English biologist Julian Huxley collected them all in his essay *The Uniqueness of Man* (1941). However, one of the most consequential distinguishing characteristics of human beings is missing in his list, as it is generally in discussions of human distinctiveness. The omission is symptomatic of the present condition of the social sciences. The malleability mentioned before as a characteristic of languages is not confined to human means of communication. It applies to human societies generally. Animal societies are, as a rule, fairly rigidly set in a species-specific mould. The group life of gorillas follows a different pattern from that of chimpanzees or gibbons. Local variations can be observed, but the basic pattern of a species' group life varies only within a very small compass. One cannot observe among animals changes of the same scope as that from a feudal to a capitalist structure or from an absolute monarchy to a multi-party republic within the time-span of a few hundred years or less. Social growth and decay, a long line of integration from one level to another, from tribe to empire and from empire to feudal disintegration, can be observed within a time-span that is short in terms of biological evolution. All these are, in fact, examples of social change within one and the same species, that of *homo sapiens*. Major changes of animal societies are biologically founded; they are signs of genetic changes. In the case of human societies a great social change such as that from tribe to empire can occur without any biological change. Representatives of different stages of social development can interbreed. And yet, such terms as evolutionism are often used indiscriminately with reference to biological evolution and to social development. The distinctiveness of the human communication in the form of speech compared with the pre-human forms centres, as I have already indicated, on its representational function. But this function is closely linked with others characteristic of the uniqueness of human beings. They are not to be found in apes or in other mammals. I will deal with them briefly in a preliminary fashion, reserving a more extensive treatment for the later text. Humans are able to hand on knowledge from generation to generation not only by means of example here and now, but above all by means of symbols which can but need not be bound to any particular time. They can thus transmit from generation to generation experiences or, in other words, knowledge which was untransmittable before simply because no uniformly recognized means of communication existed that could be acquired through learning. This is another distinguishing characteristic of the human form of communication. Languages enable humans to transmit knowledge from one generation to another and thus make it possible for human knowledge to grow. No other animal species has the natural means for knowledge increase.

The clear conceptual distinction between biological evolution and social development which has been made here with some emphasis, may seem obvious. However, much of the evidence on which this distinction rests is of fairly recent date. In the nineteenth century it was much more difficult to find significant evidence and to sift the relevant criteria which make a clear distinction between the two types of processes possible. Also, the tendency to attribute both kinds of processes to benevolent nature always acting according to human wishes and needs, was still very strong. The traumatic disappointment with the belief in a natural progress was yet to come. It came and opened the way to the recognition of the difference between social and natural processes. It took some time, and will still take some time, before it could be clearly established that the social order was an order *sui generis*. Here finally one may see the full significance of the recognition that human beings, though undoubtedly of animal descent, are not simply animals like any other, but that the continuous evolutionary process in the form of human beings has produced something new and unique.

Recognition of this fact has a bearing on the status of social sciences. It provides a firm fundament for the claim of the social sciences to a relative autonomy in relation to the biological and thus to the natural sciences. The animal heritage of humans provides a firm link of the social with the biological sciences. The latter cannot legitimize their own existence as a group of relatively autonomous sciences without reference to the process of evolution, but this process itself gave rise to a process of a different kind, to a social process not involving evolutionary changes of a genetic kind, that is, of the human species. Nature provided the matrix, but the matrix allows for changes without recognizable limits. The multitude of group-specific languages is one example of the malleability of the matrix. The multitude of human societies with different structures emerging from each other in a sequential order, in the form of a development, is another. In contrast to the evolutionary order, the developmental order is in a qualified manner reversible. Products of evolution, mammals readjusting to a life in the sea do not transform themselves into water-breathing fish. They remain air-breathing mammals. States, on the other hand, and other representatives of a relatively late stage of social development who, for one reason or another, decline can transform themselves into social units at an earlier stage of development. Their disintegration journey does not lead them necessarily to exactly the same condition from which they came. A disintegrating state is unlikely to return to a tribal condition. A disintegrating state may retain some characteristics of statehood. Instead of transforming itself into a group of tribes, the disintegrating state may, for instance, transform itself into a group of major or minor social units of a feudal type. People with a capacity for military leadership may carve out for themselves a smaller or larger territory perhaps with rivers or other landmarks favouring defence. There are many aspects of social disintegration, too many to be discussed in this context.

Communication by means of group-specific languages is one example of unique human structures emerging from within a continuous evolutionary process. Closely associated with it is another distinct human property which over time emerged from the evolutionary process: the use of sounds as a means of communication. In this case, too, humans stand in the line of succession of a long, more animalic ancestry. At the same time their way of using sounds as a medium of communication differs radically from the way animals use self-made sounds to this end. In contrast to human languages, animal sounds are not only species-specific, they are also capable of being used in a way that is radically different from the way animals use sounds as means of communication. The sounds of a language, even though they are like the sounds made by animals, used as means of communication, the manner in which they fulfil this function or, in other words, the human technique of communication, is different from that of animals using sounds as a means of communication. Animal sounds used as a kind of language lack the self-distancing aspect characteristic of human languages. Their main function is the indication of an animal's momentary condition, of its condition here and now. It is closely bound to the immediate present. They share this function with certain pre-verbal human sounds. Like the groan, the sigh, the great cry of pain, animal sounds indicate the setting of an organism, although they may have a scope for learned variations. The substance of the signals which animals give each other is not acquired through learning, but genetically determined. As a rule, moreover, sound signals which animals give each other are closely linked with other bodily movements serving as signals. The technique of communication which humans use in the form of their languages, as one may see, is very different from the animal communication by means of sounds. One need not doubt the former's descent from the latter. That is precisely the problem one encounters here. It deserves to be clearly presented. The problem is how a continuous evolutionary process can result in something totally novel and without precedent.

More shall be said later on about the unique characteristics of human languages. At the present stage of knowledge, there is no way of explaining the genesis of the human way of communication. It is difficult to imagine ways in which communication by means of more or less inborn sound signals transformed itself into communication by means of socially standardized symbols. It is at any rate of some importance to see clearly the problem presented by human language communication, even though one is not able to solve it. It must be enough to indicate the biological uniqueness of the human communication by means of changeable languages. In all likelihood, the evolutionary distance between the more animalic ancestors of humanity and the human species was considerably greater than that usually suggested if one refers to the animal descent of human beings. Moreover, the character and function of the human-made sounds we call languages as symbolic representation of the facts and functions of a really existing world is only one of several distinctly unique aspects of human communication. It is closely associated with another unique characteristic of the human methods of communication, with its changeability, with the surprising fact that the language of any particular human group can change without any demonstrable changes in the genetic constitution of their members. Eighteenth-century English is not entirely identical with twentieth-century English; nor with twentieth-century American, even if their English descent is undeniable. One encounters here a whole host of singular characteristics which distinguish human societies from the societies of other species. Not only the range of changes which gorilla sound signals can undergo is small compared with that of human beings, but also the range of changes of their whole social life. Gorillas associate with each other in ways which are characteristically different from those of chimpanzees or of gibbons.

In biological terms it is a surprising singularity of human societies that they can change their structure without any demonstrable genetic changes of their members. They can change their structure within a span of time that would be regarded as exceedingly short in the case of genetic changes from one species into another. Major changes in social structure, such as those of urbanization or of industrialization, occurred within a couple of hundred years. Perhaps it is only if one compares the relative malleability of human societies with the relative rigidity and immutability of animal societies that one becomes aware of the full weight of the problem which one encounters here. Animal societies may undergo evolu-, tionary changes, but they do not undergo social development. Not only the languages of human beings, but the whole structure of their societies can undergo development. It has become quite usual to count tool-making among the distinguishing characteristics of human beings. It is still far less usual to consider as a distinguishing human characteristic the fact that the humans can not only use, but can change tools. In a word, the development of their tool equipment is much less often seen as symptom of their singularity. In general one can say that a very wide capacity for changing their mode of life is one of the biological endowments of the human species. Perhaps its most basic aspect is the almost unlimited capacity of human groups for absorbing, storing and digesting novel experiences in the form of symbols. Not only the fact that human-made sound patterns which are socially established as symbols of specific objects or functions serve humans as their principal means of communication, deserves attention, but also the fact that the human vocal apparatus,

no native/culture divide

including its neural equipment, easily admits extensions and changes of any given fund of sound patterns. It is difficult to imagine that innovations of human groups could serve their function if the group's members could not communicate about it by means of appropriate changes in their symbol equipment. Human beings are biologically capable of changing the manner of their social life. By virtue of their evolutionary endowment they can develop socially.

II

Through the medium of languages human beings can communicate and transmit knowledge from one generation to another. A language consists of sound-patterns which, in a given society, are produced and perceived as symbols of a specific aspect of the human world. Thus the sound-pattern 'table' serves English-speaking people as a symbol of a particular piece of furniture. Primarily oral-auditory symbols, visual symbols, written or printed ones like those you are reading at this moment, have been added to them at a later stage of development. In the contemporary scheme of classification languages are often registered as items of culture. According to present ways of speaking and thinking, culture, however, can be easily understood as non-nature, if not as anti-nature. The example of languages indicates that this is a mistake. Humans are by nature specially equipped for producing and understanding sound-symbols of a language. Their vocal apparatus alone is a natural technical device of immense flexibility. Virtually the same physical apparatus can produce the thousand-and-one languages that have come and gone since Adam.

During an early phase of its growth process the human child develops the neural and motor equipment needed for language exchanges with other human beings. However, the species-specific process of growth and maturation provides a human child only with the potentials for speaking and being spoken to. Like a newly made radio station, the child's vocal and aural apparatus is now ready for use. Unlike a radio station, a child has to go through a learning process. It has to go through a learning process as a means of activating its communication potential. Its maturing species-specific equipment remains dormant and probably unusable, unless the child acquires through active interchanges and memory storage the use of a group-specific language — the language spoken by older people who care for the child. In order to become operative, the child's organic equipment has to be patterned by the articulated sound-patterns of a language spoken by other human beings. In other words, which particular set of sound-symbols first becomes engraved in the child's maturing cerebral cortex and vocal apparatus depends on the language of the society where the child grows up. From early days the processes of nature and culture intertwine. The physical condition, which enables human beings to communicate with each other by means of a language, is unequalled in the animal kingdom with regard to the wealth and diversity of the sound-combinations a human person is able to produce.

Human nature, as I have indicated before, provides only the potential for reproducing the network of sound-patterns of a given language and for understanding the data which they symbolically represent. In order to acquire a language it is necessary to activate the language potential which forms part of a human being's genetic heritage. In all likelihood, it has to be activated at the right time of the child's maturation process. Inevitably children acquire with their language aspects of the fund of knowledge of the society in which they grow up which constantly mingle with the knowledge they may acquire through their own experience. But more and more knowledge acquired as first-hand experience of a particular child and knowledge which forms part of the social fund of knowledge become closely interwoven and difficult to disentangle. From early days on, therefore, every individual experience has a language aspect. The human being becomes integrated into a universe of knowledge resulting from experiences of many other people. One's own experiences become permeated by this knowledge. One becomes integrated into this universe by learning the core of a language, by making one's own given forms of sentences or words. How can acquisition of a language achieve a newcomer's entry into the knowledge dimension of the universe? It is well worth reflecting upon the mode of existence of languages and their relations to that which they symbolically represent.

Thus by nature the maturing human person is prepared for life in the company of others with whom they can communicate, prepared for life in society. Every child has to make an individual effort to reproduce the sound-patterns used by his or her elders in their various communications. The child has to remember what these sound-patterns symbolically represent or, as one likes to say a bit more enigmatically, what these sound-patterns 'mean', and to use the remembered sound-symbols in the 'right' way, the way standardized in the society of the grown-ups. Thus the disposition to learn a language is a common property of the human species; it is species-specific. But this biological disposition leaves room for so great a variety both of the sound-patterns themselves and of whatever they symbolically represent, that the language of one human group can be completely incomprehensible to another. Thus, the specific language actually learned by a child is not species-specific, not predetermined by human nature, but society-specific, that is, predetermined by the social group within which a child grows up. By learning it, children individualize a social datum. At the same time they gain through this learning process access to the communication processes of a specific society. The extent to which human beings are by their very nature designed for life in society can be gauged from the fact that a human being, who for some reason fails to acquire a language of some kind at the right time and thus is not able to communicate or to communicate fully with other people, does not become a human being in the full sense of the word.

The briefest possible consideration of the way children acquire a language thus provides evidence which runs counter to the one-sidedly analytical tendency which has come to dominate our own manner of speaking and thinking. Concepts such as 'nature', 'culture' and 'society' are telling examples of the tendency to treat as separate entities set apart from each other problem fields at a high level of synthesis, symbolically represented by different substantives surrounded by a fog-like aura of ideological undertones. They are widely used as if they referred to aspects of this world which exist apart from each other. Thus one may, for instance, ask whether language is an aspect of nature or an aspect of culture. The advocates of this kind of intellectual apartheid can tirelessly discuss contrast problems of this type without ever examining the relationship between that which they treat as existing apart from each other. It is not difficult to find evidence for the interlocking of 'nature' and 'society' if one briefly scrutinizes the way children acquire their first language. But the dominant interest at present is directed towards either/or questions. Questions concerning the relationship or, in other words, questions of synthesis, may by comparison be regarded as marginal, as questions with little cognitive value. Yet at no moment of the processes of acquiring or using language are influences of nature or of society totally absent.

One might be tempted to speak of a wedding of nature and society or, for that matter, of nature and culture if one considers the acquisition of their first language by young children. But even that would hardly do justice to the evidence, for such a statement implies that at some period of a person's lifetime human nature and human society exist separately and at a given time begin to interact. There is no moment in the life of people who communicate by means of a language where their natural existence is in suspense, and yet one could not do justice to the evidence by diagnosing language simply as a property of human nature. What such a brief examination brings to light is the loose and ambiguous use of such concepts as human nature or, for that matter, of culture. The term 'nature' is often used today with a marked accent on the physical levels of nature, a notable underplaying of the biological and the purely speculative use of the unique characteristics of the human species. As a result, stress on the natural aspects of human languages is often dismissed as materialistic. The term 'nature' in this case is simply identified with the problem field of the physical sciences. Like culture, society too is often considered today as ontologically divorced from, if not downright antagonistic to, nature. If nothing else, the biological human potential for learning a language can indicate that this too is an error.

Many animals are biologically equipped for communication by means of sound-patterns. Only in the case of human beings do sound-patterns serving as means of communication assume the character of languages or, in other words, of social symbols which are not part of their biological equipment, but which have to be learned by every member of a group individually. Even among apes, our nearest living relatives among animals, each individual member of a group is biologically equipped with a fairly extensive armature of innate sound-patterns. They can be modified through learning and thus vary to some extent from group to group, but never sufficiently to impair the predominance of unlearned sound-patterns shared by all members of a species over local variations acquired through individual learning. In the case of human beings the evolutionary process has taken a new turn. For the first time in its course the balance between learned and unlearned sound-patterns has been reversed in favour of the former. Learned sound-patterns have acquired the dominant role, and unlearned sound-patterns and unlearned signals in general have assumed a subsidiary role. It is one of the distinguishing characteristics of the network of human sound-patterns which we call languages that only the capacity for producing learned sound-patterns, but not these patterns themselves, are genetically fixated. The sound-patterns of languages which serve humans as their principal means of communication have to be acquired through learning. They are not species-specific. These are three of the aspects which distinguish the dominant sound-patterns of humans, their languages, from the dominant signalling systems of other living beings: (a) they have to be acquired through individual learning; (b) they can vary from one society to another; and (c) they can change over time within one and the same society.

That the dominant sound-patterns by means of which people communicate with each other have to be acquired through learning and do not form part of a largely unlearned set of signals which serve animals as their principal means of communication, is one of the basic factors which endow sound-patterns of languages with the character of symbols. The expression does not mean that the symbolizing sound-patterns resemble the objects or functions which they symbolize. Language sound-patterns represent data, but they are not their likeness. Take for example the sound-pattern 'star'. Wherever English is spoken it represents the well-known luminous objects of the night sky. But the sound-pattern 'star' is totally unlike these objects. The fact that it represents these objects is solely based on a social tradition. If it were not for this tradition, one might call the bond which links the sound combination 'star' to specific cosmic objects completely arbitrary. Indeed, among French-speaking people a wholly different sound-pattern, that of 'étoile', serves as communicative symbol of these objects. So does among German-speaking groups the sound-pattern 'Stern'. People who from early days grow up in a country with a unified language, may come to feel that a natural necessity links a sound-pattern symbolically representing certain data, to these data themselves. In fact, this necessity and thus the compelling force which the sound-patterns of a language have in relation to the individual member of a tribe or a country where a given language predominates, is entirely social and human in character. Human beings could not communicate with each other if they were not habituated to the use of the same sound-patterns as symbols of the same data.

One encounters here one of the facts which shows how ill founded is the prevailing tradition which makes it appear that human nature and human society, and thus also nature and culture, belong to two ontologically different worlds which, as it were, exist independently of each other. In fact, one could make a good case for saying that languages are one of the main avenues linking nature and society or culture. Every healthy human child undergoes a genetically pre-determined, that is, natural, maturation process which from a certain stage on creates a disposition for learning to communicate with other human beings by means of the distinct sound-patterns of a language. The child's neural, motor and sensory equipment gets ready for both the sending of messages to and the reception of messages from others by means of articulated sound-waves. These sound-waves are natural or, as one sometimes says, physical data. Their articulation, which gives them the character of languages made possible by the maturing aural and vocal apparatus, is socially produced and determined.

The natural and the social, the social and the individual modes of existence of humans are inseparable; they are closely interwoven. Their interdependence is due to the unplanned and haphazard tech-nical inventiveness of the evolutionary process. The human type of communication by means of languages is based on a unique inter-twining of an unlearned biological maturation process and a social as well as individual learning process. In the case of animals, where genetically fixated, hence species-specific and unlearned, predominate over learned patterns of association as well as of com-munication, the linkage between nature and society presents no problem. The societies which ants, elephants or chimpanzees form with each other, with small adaptations to different local condi-tions, are always the same. They are species-specific, they can change only when the biological make-up or, in other words, the nature of the organisms concerned undergoes changes. To the reflecting observer the problem which the linkage between nature and society presents in the human case is more different because, among other things, human societies as well as human languages can change very drastically without any genetic changes of the human species. The solution to the problem appears to be difficult because deep-rooted habits of thought and, in particular, the habit of order-ing the world according to an old philosophical and commonsense recipe into disconnected and polarized categories such as nature and culture, meanwhile often prevents observers from seeing the obvious.

Human languages are often studied as specialized items divorced from human beings, and thus from the possibility to track down the structural characteristics which distinguish the principal human mode of communication by means of languages from the dominant animalic mode of communication by means of largely innate sets of signals, whether they have the form of specific sound-patterns or of whole-body movements. No doubt languages consist of disconnected words. Nevertheless, they have the capacity to represent connections as clearly as disconnections. One may easily overlook the obvious fact that languages consist of sound-patterns which carry messages from and to people, and which are produced and received by means of specific organic structures of the human species which can produce symbols of connections as well as of disconnections. In order to become functional these structures have to be activated and patterned during early childhood by a process of learning. In every human group with a common language a great body of interconnectable sound-patterns or, in other words, forms of speech have become socially standardized as symbols of specific objects, events, functions and other data about which the members of this group may wish to communicate with each other. Without this social standardization of specific sound-patterns as symbols of all the aspects of their world they experience as relevant to themselves, humans could not communicate or could communicate only through the attenuated residues of an earlier evolutionary stage which they still possess, that is, through largely unlearned and more situation-bound forms of communication such as groaning, laughing or crying in pain. The latter are common to the whole human species. They are produced by people more or less spontaneously in specific situations. The former, communication by means of the learned sound-patterns of a language, is also a common characteristic of the whole species. But the sound-patterns themselves, the languages, are not.

Languages follow the division of humanity into a larger or smaller variety of survival units, past or present. Most of them possess their own network of communicative sound-patterns, which are often enough totally incomprehensible to members of other human groups. Thus humans possess, together with often attenuated residues of a more animalic pre-language type of communication, a capacity for communicating by means of a language which is unique, which animals lack and which represents a post-animalic stage of evolution. Thus humans are able to discover in their own person evidence of the evolutionary process. Tradition has accustomed people to think and to speak of the relationship between animals and humans largely as if both terms referred to a more or less static ontological condition. It acts as a kind of traditional a priori; it exerts very strong pressure to present the relationship between animals and humans either as total identity or as total discrepancy. As a result, a clear answer to the problem of the relationship between animals and humans presents seemingly insuperable difficulties. One is thrown back to answers in terms of a stationary either/or. One seems to have the choice only between a wholesale reduction of the human condition to that of animals or to a mode of existence partly or wholly divorced from that of animals. Most of the familiar dualistic conceptions, such as the division of the human world into nature and culture or body and mind, are representative of this second alternative. Mind, culture or, for that matter, language, remain in that case without ontological status, without anchorage in the observable world. They are, as it were, left hanging in the air. Both these alternatives, the biologistic reductionism and the elevation of humans to an ontological position outside the natural universe, are based on the presentation as stationary conditions of what can be adequately presented only as stages in a continuous process. Human beings represent, in other words, a breakthrough of the evolutionary process to a new level. 'Post-animalic' is the significant word. While descended from animals, human beings are by nature equipped with faculties which they alone possess in the living community of the earth.

One might compare the change, not without some reservations, to the breakthrough from the level of reptiles to that of birds. In that case the transformation into wings of reptilian forelegs and beyond it the adaptation of the whole organism, opened up a new dimension for living things. An evolutionary process of very long duration gave even fairly heavy bodied animals access to the wider air space. In the case of humans, the emancipation from the dominance of genetically fixated or, in other words, of unlearned forms of experience and behaviour, and a rise to dominance in the balance of forms of experience and behaviour acquired through individual learning, endowed humans with an adaptability to changing conditions beyond the reach of their animalic forebears. An obvious illustration is the different form of adaptation to their new realm of birds and humans. Birds populated all niches of the air space which provided them with a living by means of a biological differentiation into a great number of different species. Human beings populated all niches of this earth capable of providing them with a living without biological differentiation into different species which could not interbreed, and mainly by forms of learning. In spite of a minimum of genetic adaptation, they remained a single species. All women and men, whatever their genetic differences, are capable of producing viable children.

One key aspect of the breakthrough achieved by the unplanned and aimless evolution process in the form of humans, was the new type of communication made possible by their biological organization. It reflected the dominance which the adaptation by means of learned knowledge and conduct gained in the case of humans, as well as the superiority which this dominance gave to humans in their struggles for survival. The novel technique of communicating by means of learned languages or, in other words, by means of socially determined symbols, was inherently simple.

The traditional picture of human beings is dominated by the tendency to reduce processes to antithetic stationary conditions. They are, in short, the result of a process reduction, that is, of a conceptual reduction to static conditions of sequences of events with an intrinsic dynamic which one can only observe in a state of flux. According to one alternative, human beings consist of two different components, one visible and tangible, the other invisible and intangible, such as body and mind or soul. One component, the body, has the ontological status of a natural object; the other, mind or soul, is of uncertain ontological status. In many cases they are ascribed to an imaginary spirit world. The other alternative is the reduction of human beings to the stationary condition of a body, of a physical event. In that case, humans are simply represented as animals like any others. In detail these models vary and there are many intermediary forms. What has been suggested here is, in essence, the restoration of the observable and understandable process.

The traditional a priori, the categories implanted into our modes of thinking, suggests that the world can be adequately conceived as a multitude of antitheses, such as heaven and hell, nature and culture. Yet no one seems to have thoroughly examined whether the symbolic representation of the world in the form of a multitude of stationary antitheses is really the form best suited to represent the world as it is. On closer inspection one may discover soon enough that no antithesis can adequately represent its subject matter without a complementary synthesis and, in most cases, without a processual synthesis. The antithesis nature–culture can serve as example. Both terms lack precision. One may not yet be able to say what has to be said without them. For they represent a synthesis on a very high level and such concepts are difficult to handle. Many of them are representations not of facts, but of speculations about facts or of mixtures of facts and fantasy.

The concept of nature, for instance, can symbolically represent a whole conglomerate of often diffuse and even incompatible syntheses. It can represent the great benevolent mother which produces only what is helpful and good for human beings. The term 'natural' can be used as a praise word implying that it has a high positive value in contrast to things made by humans which are artificial, not natural, and thus do not participate in the eternal goodness of nature. Also in a positive sense, the concept of nature can be used as symbolic representation of the subject matter of the physical sciences. 'The eternal laws of nature' used to be an often-heard praise word. Identification with the subject matter of physics led to the identification of nature with law-like orderliness, with quantification and with atoms or matter. But this identification of nature with matter also had a negative connotation. To attribute a high value to nature could be understood as reduction of all that exists, including the biological aspects of nature itself, to matter. Used in that sense the term 'nature' can denote the overall view of what is called materialism. Thus, the antithesis between that which is natural and that which is not given by nature but human-made, can change its value accent. In one sense objects of things which are natural could be presented as superior to objects that were human-made; in another sense natural objects were seen as inferior to human-made objects. In discussions about the relationship between nature and culture that is often the case. Nature perceived as a heap of atoms is judged as inferior compared with the high values created by human beings. As one may see, relations to facts play a relatively small part, relations to values a comparatively large part in these controversies. The term 'culture' is often nothing more than a cover for anything that is not a product of nature in the physical sense of the word.

The language of the twentieth century is rich in confused and confusing symbols of synthesis at a very high level. In other words, the overall picture and the categories on whose use the interpretation of more factual data rest, remain unclear. Today only few people are probably aware that the factual object represented by the concept of nature is almost identical with that represented by the concept of the universe — almost, for the concept of the universe includes human beings more certainly than that of nature. But the type of synthesis, often called today the type of abstraction, is different in the two cases. The concept of nature gives a stationary overall picture of the world in which we live. The concept of the universe fits more easily into a process context. The universe is often characterized as the evolving universe. Part of this process is that in its course human beings as a new class of beings emerged from our animalic ancestors. At present the conceptual equipment which society puts at our disposal is not developed enough to make humanity's emergence from within the process of the universe an easy subject of communication. But one may perhaps recognize that this is an example, one of many, which shows how a problem which in the form of a process-reducing dualism stubbornly resists a recognized solution, becomes accessible to a solution if the extraneous evaluations are abandoned and the process character is restored. The cognitive pressure for such a development is at present not strong enough. For the time being it is enough to present human beings within the framework of the universal evolutionary process as a new class of post-animalic beings. In that way one can supplement the antithesis animal/human being by means of a new look at their relationship. Recognition of the singularity of the human technique of communicating by means of a learned language neither reduces human beings to the level of animals nor removes them altogether from the evolutionary context.

That humans are derived from ape-like creatures is a commonplace. But the magnitude of this process, the evolutionary distance between common ancestors of apes and humans on the one hand and humans on the other hand, is perhaps not always realized. We may have a very clear picture of the *terminus ab quo* and the *terminus ad quem* and we have a fairly clear picture of the structural features of apes and some of our more ape-like forebears. But we know very little about the road which led from them to human beings. To register some of the features which distinguish humans from animals is not too difficult. But apart from the general mechanisms presented as levers of change, such as the struggle for survival or the survival of the fittest and the selective operation of such conditions on haphazard mutations, we know very little of the specific conditions which made more ape-like pre-human creatures communicating largely by means of species-specific signals into human beings whose principal means of communication is a language. One can easily overlook that the use of a language and, in a wider sense, the use, manipulation and storage of great numbers of symbols presupposes a specific biological equipment.

A person who at the right biological time has started to learn what is to become that person's mother tongue may, at a later stage, learn one or more other languages. But there is reason to think that a language cannot be adequately learned at a later stage, unless a first language, sound-patterns, their symbol functions and all, had become engraved in memory during the early period of a person's life biologically determined for its reception — during the period, that is, in which a child's biological maturation process first prepares it for acquiring a language. During that period a child learns that, in order to be understood by others, one has to regulate one's capacity for using one's voice and perhaps one's pleasure in using it in accordance with a social code of speaking, a common code of the older people. Only by using sound-patterns which are socially standardized as symbols of this or that, can the child be sure that the recipients experience these sounds as symbols of the same objects of communication as the sound-producing subjects. Only in that case can the child enter into a communicative dialogue with other persons. It is only in and through dialogues with others that a child develops into an individual person.

The function of human-made sound-patterns as symbols covers a wide field. Voice patterns with a symbol function can refer to simple objects such as pots and pans. Special sound-patterns may be socially stamped to indicate that the speakers refer to a deity or to themselves, to the person addressed by them or to persons absent at the time of conversation. Many present languages have sound-patterns which serve as symbols used among other things as a means of co-ordinating human activities with each other and with natural events. In short, by acquiring the skill of sending and receiving messages in the codified form of a social language, persons gain access to a dimension of the universe which is specifically human. They continue to be located in the four dimensions of space–time, like all pre-human events, but are in addition as human beings located in a *fifth* dimension, that of symbols, which serve humans as means of communication and identification. They live in a world in which everything, including all possible speakers themselves can, and among the living must, be represented by specific sound-patterns with a symbol function; in other words, they become subjects and objects of a symbol communication. Such a communication, however, demands special symbols which inform the addressee of a communication clearly about the position within the communicative figuration or in relation to it of all persons referred to in a message. One needs symbols which make it clear beyond doubt that any happening, any activities mentioned in a message refer to the sender or the sender's group itself, to the addressees or to third persons at present outside the communicative figuration. In many contemporary languages the series of personal pronouns such as I, you, he or she, we and they, symbolize this function. Thus, in a dialogue, people can be located by means of appropriate symbols as four-dimensional persons in space and time, and also as social persons, as also existing in the fifth dimension, by means of a personal pronoun and a host of other symbolic indicators of positions in that dimension.

Given the present conditions of the human world, the sound-patterns symbolically representing the position of a person within a dialogue figuration usually vary from society to society. Thus, in French, speakers identify themselves and their group by means of sound-patterns such as 'je' or 'nous-mêmes'; while English speakers would symbolically represent the same function symbolically by words as 'I' or 'ourselves'. Their unique biological organization enables human beings to represent everything which in their society can become an object of communication by means of specific sound-waves, which they can produce individually and which have been standardized as symbols of specific objects of communication socially. Objects without symbol in a particular society are not known and not knowable in that society. But there are transitional stages from the condition of not knowing to the condition of knowing in a society and vice versa. For particular objects of communication, a process of symbol making and thus of knowing or, alternatively, of symbol and knowledge decline may have got underway.

The articulated sound-waves which human beings can produce and receive as codified messages are events produced by human beings thanks to their specific neural, oral and aural equipment. This equipment enables humans not only to produce and receive sound-waves as raw material of messages, it also enables them to articulate and, more generally, to fashion the sound-waves produced by themselves in a great variety of different ways — a variety which appears to be physically and biologically without limits, but which is kept socially within specific boundaries by means of social standardization and unification without which sound-pattern symbols produced by humans could not fulfil their function as means of communication within a given society. At any given time limits are set in every society to the range of communication by the fact that the social fund of knowledge available in any human society and thus the standardized language symbolically representing all possible experiences within that society, have very definite boundaries, even though some of its members may be at work to extend these boundaries. However, the range of knowledge or, in other words, of experiences available in a society and symbolically represented by its language, which covers all overt or covert topics of communication, is further limited by the structure of a given society and particularly by its power relations. They play a considerable and often a decisive part, not only in what is standardized as symbolic means of communication within a given society, but also in the emotional and evaluative undertones associated with many language symbols and generally in the mode of standardization.

At present it may still sound a bit unfamiliar if one says that a language is a web of human-produced sound-patterns which have developed in a particular human group and have come to be standardized there, mainly by its use itself, by the need to avoid misunderstandings, as symbols of specific topics of communication. Both sounds and symbols can change over time, though rarely without some continuity, in connection with changes in the group's fortunes and experiences.

III

A more familiar way of referring to the symbol-function of these human-made sound-patterns is that of presenting their function as the *meaning* of language components such as sentences or words. The concept of meaning, however, is far from simple. It has come to be used in learned discourse of the twentieth century as a keyword of a philosophical mystique. In that sense the meaning, whether of speech or of other actions, is often treated as if this term referred to an ultimate, a totally autonomous region of the individual existence. One may think of Max Weber's emphasis on the meaning which an action has for the individual actor. Yet, an individual action rarely stands on its own. It is usually oriented to actions of other persons. As a rule, the meaning of an action for the actor is codetermined by the meaning it may have for others. People's relationships with each other are not additive. Society has not the character of a heap of individual actions comparable to a heap of sand, nor that of an anthill of individuals programmed for mechanical co-operation. It rather resembles a web of living persons who, in a great variety of ways, are dependent on each other. The drives and feelings, the standards and the actions of one person may reinforce those of

NB

others or deflect them from their initial aim. They may share the same code of conduct and yet be opponents. Verbal disputes can serve as example. If the disputants do not speak the same language, they cannot engage in a verbal dispute. They can hit or kill each other. But a combat fought out with the weapons of words requires that someone, who may be an interpreter, speaks the languages of both sides.

It is one of the distinguishing characteristics of the principal human form of communication that every language, for the time being, is spoken and understood only by a limited section of the human species. Yet, these limiting boundaries go hand in hand with an apparently unlimited capacity of many languages for extension, for verbal innovations, if the field of knowledge grows. In both respects the main human form of communication by means of languages contrasts sharply with the main form of animal communication. The latter is to a far higher extent genetically fixed, hence largely identical, for a whole species, though local variations may exist, and too rigid to embody innovations. The human form of communication by means of a learned language represents a unique evolutionary innovation. There is nothing like it in the whole animal kingdom. It is based on the final breakthrough in the balance between learned and unlearned, genetically fixed forms of conduct in favour of the former. The final shift in this balance was preceded and, no doubt, was made possible, by a very long preparatory evolutionary change in the same direction. But although in its course the ability of organisms to adapt their conduct to changing situations in the light of experiences acquired through individual learning and stored in one's memory tracts, steadily increased, unlearned, genetically programmed forms of conduct and thus of communication retained the upper hand. On balance, they still dominate the self-regulation and thus the adjustment to changing situations of the living species of apes. In the case of humans, the rise to dominance of learned types of communication in the form of languages, in all likelihood identical with what is known as cortical or cerebral dominance in the case of the human brain, represented a breakthrough as great, if not greater in terms of the evolutionary innovation than was necessary to enact it, as that, say, which led before from terrestrial reptiles to airborne birds.

Communication by means of a language can serve as an example of the unity in diversity characteristic of humankind. All human beings use a language as their main form of communication. Which language they use depends on the society where they grow up and live. At present the diversity of languages is considerable. If the present trend towards integration of smaller into larger social units retains its impetus, which is by no means certain, the diversity of languages may diminish. A world language, a lingua franca of humanity, may emerge. But whether or not that will happen, language communication is one of the distinguishing marks of the human species. A clearer view of the structure and development of language communication can help towards a more realistic assessment of that which separates humans from those of their ancestors still firmly bound to the precedence of largely innate pre-language signals. At present people seem to be generally inclined to treat human nature and human society as if these terms referred to totally separate compartments of the human existence. Also, the lack of a theory of social symbols is one of the major factors which contributes to a misunderstanding of the evolutionary distance between human beings and their more animalic ancestors.

A brief glance at the mechanics of human language communication can show clearly enough the interwovenness of biological and social factors in the acquisition and use of a language. The fact that human babies not only can but must learn a language, if they are to become fully developed human beings, has already been mentioned. It is fairly obvious. So is the fact that human beings are biologically fitted for language communication with others and thus for life in society. If the human image underlying many philosophies and not a few theories of the human sciences gives the impression that every human being is by nature fitted for living alone as an isolated individual, it may well be that characteristics of the social habitus dominant in the more developed societies of our time and the basic categories of thinking connected with it blind the eyes to what is obvious.

Many idiomatic phrases bear witness to an uneven I–We balance, tilted in favour of the 'I'. Thus, in fact, a baby learns a language which is the medium of communication in a particular society. But the phrase 'learning a language' is usually reserved for people beyond the baby stage who learn a second or a third language. If one refers to a baby, one usually does not say the child is learning a language; one prefers to say 'the child is learning to speak'. The blend of natural maturation and social learning is in this case more strongly balanced in favour of the former. Or take the expression the 'meaning of words' as a turn of phrase; it is not strictly correct.

For a sound-pattern is not a word if it has not a meaning or, expressed differently, if it has not received the social imprint as a symbol of a specific topic of communication. Take the sound-pattern 'abracadabra'. It is not a word, because it does not bear the stamp of a human group which makes it understandable for all its members as the symbol of a specific object or function. It is a meaningless sound. By habitually saying words have a meaning one is in effect asserting that a sound-pattern with a meaning has a meaning. One presents the symbol-functions of language components as a kind of property of the latter and perhaps even as a property which every speaker of a language has given to its sentences and words individually. In that version the relationships between word, meaning and the intended object or function of the latter remain utterly obscure. The traditional and thus decidedly more idiomatic way of speaking enjoins us to distinguish between languages and their components, such as sentences or words on the one hand, their meanings on the other hand and, thirdly, the meant objects or functions of communication. This blocks the way, amongst other things, to a full understanding of the fact that, in the form of a language, nature and society or, if one prefers, nature and culture, are firmly locked into each other.

A fuller understanding demands a small but indispensable step which may perhaps be difficult. Instead of distinguishing between language components and their meanings produced by human beings, one can pursue a more reality-congruent track only if one inserts the analytical scalpel in the first place between sound-patterns and their symbol-functions. At a later stage one may then examine the relationship between these symbols and the objects or functions of communication which they symbolically represent.

The sound-pattern of a language component is a physical event. It is in the first place usually produced by a human being as a means of sending a message to other human beings. The sound-pattern produced by a human being is the physical carrier of the message. It has more or less the same function. It might be more correct if one considers the sound-pattern of a word as the actual carrier of a message, like the movements of telephone wire or the radio-waves emitted by a sender and re-transformed into whatever sound-patterns the people at the sending radio station wish to transmit to the listeners with their receivers. The sending of a radio message would be a futile exercise if no one's receiving apparatus was tuned to the wavelength on which the radio message has been sent. How can human beings who send to others a message by stirring up articulated sound-waves be sure that their messages will be received by other human beings? They have a chance to be received only if those who send a spoken message and those who are expected to be the receivers of the message speak the same language or, in other words, if the sound-patterns produced by the sender of the message symbolically represent for the receiver of the message the same objects or functions which they represent for the sender of the message. Thus, if the shouted message 'A small herd of buffaloes is coming in the direction of the old trees on your right-hand side', is to fulfil its task, sender and receiver of the message must associate the same topics of communication with sound-patterns such as 'a small herd of buffaloes' or 'the old trees on your right-hand side'. A language can only function as such if individuals throughout a former or present survival unit use and understand the same sound-patterns as symbolic representations of the same topics of communication.

This is uniformly achieved through education. As a rule children learn early in life to remember which topics of communication specific sound-patterns in their society symbolically represent. They learn to regulate their own speech behaviour and, indeed, their own behaviour generally in accordance with the common code of producing and receiving articulated sound-patterns as messages for and from other people which prevails in their society. This is the crucial aspect of the interlocking of nature and society in the structure of human languages. For the purposes of communication the production and reception of voice-sounds, a purely organic or physical event, is no longer subjected mainly or exclusively to the bondage of genetic fixating. Instead, the organic event of voice-production, to a large extent, can be patterned in accordance with a learned social code of voice regulation which most members of a language society have made their own when young, and which makes it possible for them to understand the same sound-patterns as symbols of the same objects and functions of communication. One could perhaps speak of humanity's *symbol emancipation*, its liberation from the bondage of largely unlearned or innate signals and the transition to the dominance of a largely learned patterning of one's voice for the purposes of communication.

At present we know very little about the conditions and the manner in which this breakthrough to communication by means of socially standardized symbols has been achieved. One can only see the fact that it has been achieved and that it represented an evolutionary innovation as great and consequential, if not more consequential, than the transformation of reptilian forelegs into wings. The relative perfection which language communication achieved in the *sapiens* type of hominids was hardly the result of a single mutative spurt. One may think of a long process, a sequence of smaller spurts in the same direction, each providing its own rewards for those endowed with it in terms of advantages for the continuous struggle of the species. If one now looks back at the change from the type of largely unlearned communication prevailing among animals to the largely learned language communication prevailing among humans, as if it were a single event, it is not too difficult to recognize in passing some of these advantages. Unlearned animal signals, whether voice-signals or whole-body movements, are much more rigidly tied to the momentary situation of the signalling animal. It would be very difficult to teach dogs to bark as if they felt angry with someone perceived as intruder, if they did not perceive the situation as circumstances requiring their barking signal. Apes may be innately endowed with a very large repertoire of postures, movements and sounds. They may even be able to learn variations of their innately fixed signals as a means of adjusting their communications to each other more closely to changing circumstances. No signal of theirs approaches changing conditions as closely in details as the information that a small herd of buffaloes is approaching on the right-hand side in the direction of some visible old trees. Human speech behaviour presupposes in more than one respect a comparatively high capacity for distancing oneself from one's own momentary situation. One can speak of the moon even if it is not visible, of a small herd of buffaloes not yet in sight. Orientation with the help of sentences and words permits a flexibility in one's adjustment to changing situations quite beyond the reach of animals, whose genetic make-up may provide an excellent way of coping with a specific situation and yet block their ability to cope with the demands of their situation if the task changes in a manner for which a species is not genetically equipped.

IV

In the essay, *The Uniqueness of Man*, mentioned before, published in 1941 and well worth reading again, Julian Huxley observed that the swings of the pendulum in people's opinion about their position among the animals, have been too great in either direction. A time in

which the human connection with animals was only dimly perceived, was followed by a period in which biologists were inclined to
perceive only similarities between animals and humans and to overlook differences between them. One of his examples of the relative
rigidity of innate animal behaviour may be of use in this context. A
mother bird may feed her young when they gape and squeak in the
nest (Huxley, 1941:20). But if they have been ejected from the nest
by a young cuckoo, she lets her own young starve and feeds the
young cuckoo in her nest. Her genetic make-up prepares her for
feeding gaping and squeaking young fledglings in her nest, but she
cannot adjust to the unfamiliar situation of having to put food into
open beaks on the ground. In the same way, female baboons whose
offspring have died will continue carrying the corpses until they
have not merely putrefied but mummified. This appears to be due to
a contact stimulus: the baboon mother will react similarly to any
moderately small and furry object. Examples such as these may help
towards a better understanding of the evolutionary innovation
represented by humans, of the breakthrough they represent into a new
realm — that of symbols as a means of orientation and of steering
behaviour. What humans can do and what animals as far as we
know cannot do, is symbolic analysis and symbolic synthesis of
changes in a familiar situation and a corresponding change of
behaviour. The hen bird genetically equipped with an urge to feed
her young in the nest cannot perform the symbolic anaylsis and the
symbolic synthesis necessary in order to grasp that her young ejected
from the nest by the young cuckoo gape and squeak now from the
ground. Nor is the steering of her behaviour versatile and elastic
enough for her to change behaviour in the light of the new analysis
and synthesis of the situation by means of symbols.

The symbol character of people's means of communication with
each other and with themselves has so far hardly found the attention it deserves. This is partly due to the fact that the sound-pattern
aspect of human means of communication is treated as negligible
and is often enough completely neglected. But it is also due in part to
a commonsense theory backed by public opinion. It covers sufficient ground to silence further questions. According to it concepts
are formed by a mental process of abstraction and generalization. A
person arrives, so it seems, at concepts such as table or tree by
abstracting from all properties which make specific trees or tables
different and by retaining only those properties which all trees,
all tables, have in common. As an approach to the problem of

concept-formation it recommends itself not only by its simplicity, but above all by the fact that it presents concept-formation as a neat mental process of a single human individual. As such it easily falls in line with a well-known pattern: concept-formation can be seen as an individual mental process with a firm beginning in the course of time and possibly with an end.

One of the difficulties of this commonsense theory is that it cannot be easily matched with observations. If one tries to do that one recognizes soon enough that the explanation of concepts in terms of an individual mental process of abstraction and generalization is a typical example of a single-person reduction of data which require explanation in terms of the interweaving of actions and mental processes of many people. That an individual mental process of abstraction enables a person to launch an entirely new concept is certainly not an event which one can encounter very frequently. Even if it does occur, such an individual mental process alone is never enough to account for the presence in a language of any concept attached to a specific sound-pattern. It can attain this character only when it has gone through the mill of dialogues involving and interweaving the mental activities of many people. This interweaving of the activities of many members of a group is in human terms, and thus sociologically, a crucial aspect of the fortunes of a concept in any particular language and it is rather questionable whether these activities have predominantly the character of abstraction and generalization. In many cases what may appear at first sight as transition to a higher level of abstraction and generalization, reveals itself on closer inspection as the transition to a higher level of synthesis.

One encounters here one of the basic differences between a traditional philosophical and a sociological approach, especially between the philosophy and sociology of knowledge. The basic model of a human being underlying the mainstream of the European philosophy of knowledge is that of a person who acquires knowledge alone and all by him- or herself. However, every theory of concept-formation which is based on this model of a human being encounters the same difficulty. In order to serve as means of communication specific sound-patterns must be understood in the same sense by a whole group of people. It is difficult to imagine how the relative identity of language within a group of people can ever be ensured without a modicum of social integration and control.

How can persons who form concepts individually and all by

themselves, concepts which they send by means of sound-patterns or, in more recent times also by means of visual patterns to other persons, ever be sure that the sensory patterns activate in the memory store of the messages' recipients the same dormant pictures which the sender of the message associates with these sound-patterns? The human form of acquiring knowledge in the form of a language can be understood only if one takes into account both receivers and senders of messages. The philosophical tradition tends to give knowledge the appearance of a sender's monologue. The individual person as subject of knowledge faces in that case the enigma of objects alone and tries to solve it without reference to other persons each of whom seems to be in a similar position. The task ahead is to restore to knowledge its character as at the same time both knowledge of objects which are faced by each person individually and objects of language communication between them. Human beings are by nature endowed with an unlimited capacity for producing and receiving sound-patterns which can serve as symbols of every possible object of communication within a group. What cannot be represented by the web of symbols of a specific human group, is not known to its members. Being by nature endowed with the capacity for orienting themselves in the world by means of language symbols, they are also in need of symbols; they must acquire the symbols of a group whatever its sensory pattern may be. They cannot regulate their behaviour, in short, cannot become human without learning a language.

Our forebears, who could not have known all that is known today, would have been in an unbearable position had not another unique propensity of their nature come to their help, a vastly extended capacity for conjuring up from feelings or experiences in their memory stores and representing symbolically things or events which at this and perhaps at any instant were not there and may never have existed. They could form fantasy images representing objects of which no reality-congruent image was at hand.

It was only in the twentieth century that human beings developed their knowledge of the sun to the point where one can say that human knowledge is reasonably reality-congruent. Our forebears often formed fantasy pictures of the sun to fill the gap of their knowledge. But the replacement of fantasy knowledge by more realistic knowledge poses a peculiar problem. Emotionally fantasy knowledge can take deep roots in the lives of human groups. It can give to such an extent the impression of being reality-congruent that

The way concepts came into being – The bacillus

it blocks the search for more reality-congruent symbols. The philosophical theory of knowledge itself can serve as example. By placing the mental process of an isolated individual into the centre of the knowledge problem, by postulating that concept-formation originates in such individual mental processes as those of abstraction and generalization, philosophical theories of knowledge are able to find an answer to a problem whose solution had become a deeply felt need of human beings. Many philosophers themselves are inclined to believe that the need to answer this question is laid on in the human intellect a priori, or in other words, prior to all individual experience and thus by human nature itself.

The need in question is that for explanations of events in terms of causes and thus of beginnings. Theories of concept-formation in terms of abstraction and generalization satisfy this need. They provide an answer as to how concepts begin and at least the hope of an eventual answer to the question how they can be explained. One can say, for example, the concept 'bacillus' was created during the first part of the nineteenth century by a German scientist named Müller. He recognized as originators of illnesses some objects which under the microscope looked like little sticks. Generalizing his own experience he put forward the hypothesis that many illnesses are caused by beings which looked like little sticks. By borrowings from the Latin language he coined the word 'bacillus'. As it turned out soon enough, not all bacilli looked like little sticks, but the term took root in most contemporary langauges and has done good service as a means of orientation ever since. It represented a new answer to the question how certain types of illnesses begin and what or who causes them. The story, briefly told, also provides some confirmation for the theory of abstraction and generalization as explanation of the way concepts come into being.

There are several ways in which concepts can gain currency in a human group. Take the word 'father'. It is an example, small but thought provoking, of a beginningless process. One of its major roots was, according to the Oxford dictionary, a common Teutonic language. That raises the question of its cause or beginnings there and so on ad infinitum. It refers to a characteristic human relationship which in animal societies may be hardly distinguished from other relationships. As such, it has come to be socially standardized for one's progenitor, probably in accordance with the changes of the kin group relationship from a larger to a smaller male-dominated formation. Children do not use this sound-pattern as a result of an individual mental process founded on the observation that other children stand in the same relationship to their fathers as each of whom stands individually to her or his own male parent by way of abstraction, but because they learn early that the expression 'father', or a corresponding expression, is used in their society with reference to this special relationship between humans. As far as one can look back the term was used in connection with special duties and rights. The same goes for the concept 'sun'. It can be used in an English-speaking society by children as well as by astronomers. The aura of associations may be different in the two cases, but the core or the message which this sound-pattern carries within such a society from one person to another will be the same because this sound-pattern has been socially stamped with this message. Both might be stumped if they were asked to look at 'le soleil'.

A standard example for the development of concepts is the word 'to develop'. It shows briefly one of the main directions in which concepts can develop. Today we employ as a matter of course many substantives with a global connotation and not immediately intelligible to any tangible event. If one examines such sound-patterns one can usually find that they are derived from sound-pattern symbols of more limited range which refer to more immediately tangible objects or events. The latter are often called 'concrete concepts', the former 'abstractions'. But concrete concepts do not exist. Pots and pans may be called 'concrete objects'. But the concept of a pot cannot be said to be concrete. Nor is it abstract. Applied to concepts the conceptual polarity concrete/abstract is unusable. What can be observed are concepts representing a lower level of synthesis, others representing a higher level of synthesis. The development of the 'abstractions' in the language of societies at the presently highest stage of development often shows this character, of the development from a lower to a higher level of synthesis. The concept 'development' itself can serve as example. As late as in the seventeenth century the standardized message of the sound-pattern 'to develop' would still be understood if one said that one wished to take off the wrappings of a baby. Towards the end of the nineteenth century 'to develop' could still be representative of a middle range synthesis. It could mean for example the gradual opening out one's troops for an attack. The social need for a communicable conceptual representation of continuous gradual growth in the direction towards greater differentiation evidently increased. The social process of thinking had reached a stage where a common symbol for a gradual unfolding, a continuous and often self-perpetuating process of differentiation from within was needed whatever external levers of change in the same direction may combine with the internal dynamics. The term 'development' assumed this function. The example is telling because the counterpart to the verb 'to develop', the verb 'to envelop', did not undergo a corresponding change: it still retains in a highly specialized way its lower synthesis form, for instance if one speaks of the envelope of a letter. At present the concept 'development' is so little developed that one does not yet know very much about the conditions under which a concept develops in a specific direction. (Nor has the term 'regression' fully assumed its significance as symbol for a change in the opposite direction.) But it is perhaps noteworthy that in one specific field the term 'to develop' is still used in its older form, in the field of photography. One may develop a film.

The change in the social function of the term 'to develop' shows a characteristic pattern. It is a pattern which one often encounters in languages with many components at a high level of synthesis. As has been mentioned before, they all are derived from sound-symbols at a lower level of synthesis or, as one likes to say, from something less abstract or more concrete. People who, professionally or not, are used to the handling of concepts at a high level of synthesis, differentiation and reality-congruence are often inclined to attribute this capacity to the quality of their own intellect alone and undoubtedly that quality plays a part in their capacity for handling such concepts. One may overlook that the possibility to manipulate concepts at a high level in all these respects depends on the overall development of concepts in that society.

One has the impression — our knowledge is too incomplete to say more — that a great spurt in that direction occurred among the ancient Greeks in pre-Classical and Classical times. In that case, too, advances in conceptual synthesis, analysis and reality-congruence went hand in hand. To know more exactly what happened one would have to make comparative studies with Egyptian, Babylonian and what little is known of other contemporary languages, especially of the Phoenician language. The same can be said of the period usually called today the late Middle Ages and the Renaissance. Their representatives benefited from the conceptual innovations of antiquity and went beyond them. In the nineteenth and particularly the twentieth centuries concept development has assumed more than ever before the characteristics of a partly self-

A Whorffian view of language.

perpetuating knowledge development. Prior to that period not very many societies passed through a phase where their members experienced the need to communicate with each other about the development of their society or of societies in general. In the last resort it is always the fortune of a society, its changing social structure and its changing position among other societies, which is reflected in the development and character of its language. A people's language itself is a symbolic representation of the world as the members of that society have learned to experience it during the sequence of their changing fortunes. At the same time a people's language affects their perception and thus also their fortune.

One approaches here one of the strangest singularities of the way human beings, compared with other species, experience their world. They experience it not only as the old theories of knowledge suggested, as subjects facing objects, but as subjects facing the physical world of the objects themselves, the houses, the mountains, the plants and the sun, and at the same time through the medium of their communication with each other, through the medium of their language. For, although the primary function of language is that of a means of communication, language communication colours the whole mode of experience of human beings. One may be tempted to represent the basic human situation to which I am referring here in a manner approaching that of the traditional theories of knowledge. It is not suggested here, however, that language interposes itself like an irremovable veil between subjects and objects. The sun which rises above the horizon early in the day is the real sun radiating what humans sense as light and as warmth. At the same time, we experience the rising and setting of the sun in terms of a language, in terms of our communication with each other. With their help one can refer to the sun whether it is visible or not. At the same time humans are well able to distinguish between the concept of the sun and the sun itself, between the symbol and that which it symbolizes. The tendency towards polarization and reduction may mislead the observer.

As a process language is in a condition of flux. The balance between the feeling or fantasy content and the reality-congruence of a symbol can change in either direction. The character of language components as symbols is closely connected with the greatly extended human capacity to evoke by means of a sound-pattern memory images of objects or events which are not present when the evocation takes place. The sounds can evoke such an image irrespective of whether or not the topic of communication represented by it occurs here and now. The language provides specific sound-patterns symbolically indicating their presence or their absence. As humans normally grow up with a specific language, their mother tongue, they usually develop a strong feeling of a natural connection, a kind of necessity binding to each other social sound-pattern, social symbol function and the object of communication itself which they symbolically represent. In fact, no necessity of this kind exists. The English sound-pattern 'sun', the French sound-pattern 'soleil' and any number of different sound-patterns in different languages symbolically represent the same thing with equal ease. Except in a few cases such as mama, cuckoo, murmur and similar words which may represent a musical imitation of a natural event, the relationship between sound, symbol and symbolized object or function can be regarded as purely fortuitous. In point of fact no natural necessity of this kind exists, but a kind of social necessity can be detected. The linkage has in many cases a long and, as far as one can see, beginningless ancestry. It is the present outcome of a society's long development. Anybody who tried to break the linkage would not be understood by his or her fellows. Such a person might seem to speak a foreign language or gibberish.

The constellation of languages or of different versions of the same language, reflects the power structure of a society or a group of societies. If different languages or different versions of the same language are spoken in the same society, they usually rank in accordance with the power- and status-chances of the groups concerned. But that is not all. A language itself exerts power upon its individual speakers. It has a force of its own, which more or less compels all speakers of that language to subordinate their individual self-regulation in speaking it to the communal speech-regulations of that language. How can that be? Is not a language simply the sum total of the speech behaviour and thus of the self-regulation in speaking of the individuals composing a group? The answer is simple and obvious. Individual members of a group with a common language usually have a certain margin for deviating from the traditional regulating conventions governing speech behaviour in a group. This margin keeps a language in a condition of flux. It opens the way to limited changes in a group's stock of symbols and thus offers opportunities for new symbols to develop in response to new communal experiences. They can emerge from within the numerous and almost incessant dialogues between group members and thus without breaking the continuity of the language flow. But if the margin of individual deviation from the conventional stock-in-trade of sound-symbols becomes too great, the individuals concerned will simply no longer be understood by their fellows. That is the answer to the question why in every human group speaking a language of its own, individuals have to subordinate their self-regulation in speaking to the social regulations of their communal language. If they do not, the possibility to communicate with each other via a language is brought to a standstill. Language becomes in that case, as it quite often does, a barrier to, rather than a means of, communication.

Limits to the margin of individual speech deviation can also serve as a reminder that a language is not the sum total of individual acts of speaking within a group. Nor is it simply a code of general rules or laws, showing the right and the wrong way of speaking in a particular society. The network of interwoven sound-patterns, symbolically representing everything communicable and knowable in a particular society, is a tangible and substantial item. The question of how the symbol-network of a language came to emerge from more animalic, pre-language forms of communication among ancestors of the present human groups and how it developed into a great number of different languages, represents the present frontier of human knowledge.

One can surmise that the capacity for communication by means of the sound-symbols of a language has a high survival value. All ancestral forms of humanity not fully equipped for language communication have vanished. Among the existing human groups, extensive sets of sound-symbols covering everything that is communicable are handed on from generation to generation and may change in transit as part of a largely unplanned long-term process. From it a set of general rules or principles known as grammar can usually be abstracted. But it is not as if such laws of languages had been established in the manner of a social contract by a group of respectable citizens tired of the Tower-of-Babel-like linguistic disorderliness around them. Attempts at a kind of linguistic legislation have certainly been made from time to time: in France the once royal Académie, in Germany a book widely accepted as authoritative, *die Duden*, are examples. But they are at the most secondary reinforcements of the primary order of languages. The latter is simply due to the function of languages as means of communication within specific social units. The regularities of languages, of which those called their grammar are an example, established themselves in the first instance in and through their practical use as part of an unplanned process of social development of which no absolute beginning is known or even imaginable.

For a very long time human languages must have grown without much reflection as part of a self-evident convention. Most people accept as a matter of course the sound-patterns which in their society serve as symbols of specific objects of communication. At the most, specialists regard the relationship between object and its sound-symbol as a matter of reflection. Native speakers of a language often cannot help feeling that their sound-symbol for any object of communication is the right, the 'natural' one. Moreover, even sound-symbols of so uncontroversial an object as the sun can have different undertones in different languages. Almost every noun with a reasonably long career has a specific aura in a specific language. French people usually understand without difficulty the idiomatic phrase 'le roi soleil'. A literal translation into German or English might sound a little odd. Translators know how great these differences can be. Idiomatic use of a language not one's own presents many pitfalls.

Perhaps it requires an effort of self-distancing to realize that the relationship between the sound-patterns serving as symbols of certain objects and these objects themselves is in most cases, if not in all, a matter of convention and, in that sense, fortuitous. But, none the less the feeling of a necessary relationship between the two in one's native language is not entirely unjustified. In societies like ours where the term 'necessity' is often pre-empted by associations with physical or natural types of necessity, it may not always be easy to distinguish clearly between natural and social types of necessity. There is no natural necessity linking the sound-pattern 'sun' to the object in the sky which it symbolically represents, but there may be a certain social necessity for linking the two. One may not be understood if one uses another word. The problem area one enters here at present is not an area which attracts much reflection and research. Yet attention to the triangular relationship between language sound-patterns as physical carriers of messages, as symbols of objects of communication and these objects themselves opens the door to a problem-field of great promise. At present it is still to some extent blocked by a convention of long standing, according to which related problems are usually discussed in terms of a subject–object relationship.

V

Linguistic usages can generate the strongest resistance against advances in knowledge and reasoning about the world in which we live. It is quite customary in our age to speak of *language, reason* and *knowledge* as if each of these three nouns referred to a separate and independent realm of human existence. There are specialists who proceed as if each of them could be explored without regard for the others. Theories of language and theories of knowledge, for instance, often give the impression that their subject matter existed in different worlds. Their relationship is an open question not very often drawn into the limelight of an explicit discussion. Yet, if one changes in each of these cases from the substantival to the verbal form and considers the relationship between three sets of human activities called *to speak, to think*, and *to know*, the separation and isolation of each of these fields becomes much more questionable. On closer inspection one may recognize that all three activities are concerned with the handling of symbols. It is hard to keep them apart. People who speak send messages to others by means of sound-waves articulated in accordance with the models of a communal language, knowledge of which they expect to share with potential receivers of the message. Thinking is today widely regarded as a highly individualized human activity. Attention is often focused exclusively on acts of thinking, performed in silence and perhaps in solitude by a single person, while even today acts of thinking by way of discussions, of thinking in groups, are frequent events. Children are more inclined than adults to think aloud. In fact, thinking in silence and without any overt form of speaking has to be learned. Whether and how far it is a standard requirement of a grown-up person depends on the stage of development of the society in which a person grows up and lives. In earlier stage societies thinking in groups, on balance, is likely to prevail over silent soliloquy. The trend towards thinking without overt acts of speaking has been greatly reinforced by the spread of literacy. In more developed societies the ability to read without overtly using one's voice-producing muscles is a standard requirement for adults. I still remember sitting for a while in what was then the Reading Room of the British Museum next to a learned elderly Asian gentleman, who in a low voice spoke to himself what he read. It was one of those well-remembered seminal experiences which helped me to realize that the voiceless forms of thinking and reading corresponded to a specific stage of social and individual development.

A tradition of long standing and linguistic usages connected with it have created the impression that thought, knowledge and language existed, as it were, in different compartments of a human being. Studies and theories of thinking or, according to taste, of reason and studies and theories of language, accordingly, appear as two totally separate fields of exploration and as the professional task of different and independent groups of specialists. In accordance with the traditional academic division of labour which goes back at least to the Middle Ages and probably much further, the human propensity of thinking in its various guises such as reason, mind, rationality, reflexion or intellect is widely considered as a human universal. It is regarded as essentially identical in all human groups and at all periods of time as long as human beings exist. Reason, mind or whatever name one chooses to give for this supposedly unvarying human property, can therefore appear to be at variance with language, which may change from society to society and from age to age. Reason or mind may also seem to be different from knowledge, which can grow throughout the ages or, as the case may be, decay. One cannot help feeling that the linguistic and conceptual heritage leaves us here with a divided and somewhat confused human image. Can it be that linguistic custom, in this respect as in others, makes it all too easy to rest content with analysis without synthesis, with using assorted nouns such as language, mind and knowledge for different aspects of the human person, each of which seems to make good sense in its own compartment? Why bother about their connections within the more or less well integrated unity of a human person?

Separation of the three nouns is easy enough if one regards them as symbols of three different fields of studies whose exploration is the professional task of different groups of specialists. Separation becomes more difficult if one considers these nouns as symbols of different sets of functions interconnected within the overall frame of reference of a human person. In the former case enquiries such as those of reason or mind may easily become a playground for speculation. At a time when reason was still a fashionable word, Kant imputed to it a structure prior to all experience and thus independent of all learned knowledge including knowledge of a language. At a time when reason had ceased to be a philosophical term of fashion and mind had to some extent taken its place, Lévi-Strauss again attributed to mind a structure prior to all learned knowledge. One could probably diminish confusion if one would not fasten on any particular type of relationship as the universal characteristic of human experience, but on the making of connections as such. If one goes beyond that one is in danger of attributing to mind, or for that matter, to language and knowledge, specific unlearned properties — properties *a priori* — structures which in fact are due to their common social functions as means of communication and orientation.

Take as an example the social function performed in languages such as modern Dutch, French, German or English by a series of personal pronouns. One may venture to say that human languages everywhere, in all likelihood, have or had grammatical forms serving the function performed by personal pronouns in the languages mentioned. But most certainly not all of them used a series of special words such as we, you or they in order to perform these functions. In Latin for instance, special verbal forms performed this function. Indicating the reference to the first person the ancient Romans said 'amo' where contemporary English people say 'I love'. But whatever the symbolic form may be by means of which those who speak a language seek to perform it, the function itself and thus this structural element of languages, has its root not in language or mind as such, but in the fact that living together in groups makes certain elementary demands and, moreover, the same demands on people who, in order to live with each other, must be able to communicate with each other by means of symbols. Thus the personal pronoun 'I' or an equivalent symbol is used in a conversation in order to indicate that the activity mostly represented by a verb has been, is being, or is to be performed by the speaker him- or herself. The singular 'you' carries the message that an activity mentioned in the communication refers to the person addressed. A we-form indicates that a group including the speaker is involved, while third-person statements refer to people who are at the time of speaking absent, not involved or, at any rate, are neither the speaker nor the addressed person.

Social situations which make it necessary for communicating people to express clearly whether items of their message refer to themselves, to the addressed person, to a third person in the singular or the plural, arise again and again in the life and thus the experience of human groups. The structure of the language reflects in this case very clearly not the nature of human beings nor the individual person seen in isolation, but human beings in society. It reflects the recurrent social need to express clearly in a socially standardized symbolic form the position in relation to the sender and receiver of a message to which the message refers. It is in this case thus very clearly the figuration of people involved in sending and receiving a message, and their positions within the figuration, which structures language. It is not enough to seek structures in language, thought or knowledge as if they had an existence of their own independently of the human beings who speak, think or know. In all these cases one can connect characteristics of the structure of language, thought or knowledge with the functions they have in and for the life of human beings in groups.

If the social frame of reference is restored, it becomes easier to perceive the unreality of all tendencies to see each of the three functions to which the three nouns refer in isolation. What would language be if one had no knowledge to speak about? What would knowledge and thought be if they could not be transmitted from person to person by means of the sound-symbols of a language? Worst afflicted by the tendency to isolate without considering connections, to divide without scrutinizing relationships, is probably the human propensity to think. For centuries the linguistic usage which enables people to refer to this and related cerebral functions by means of reifying nouns such as reason or mind, has played havoc among the learned. It has given rise to a number of rather idiosyncratic mythologies in which symbols such as these acted the part played in the older type of myth by gods or spirits. Indeed, the German term 'Geist', probably related to the English word 'ghost', makes it possible to represent both types of myth by means of the same symbol. Hegel's fame rests on his highly imaginative and indeed immensely intelligent philosophy centred on the development of the 'Geist'. In the English language the term 'mind' can be broadly used as equivalent of the German Geist. The *Oxford English Dictionary* mentions as one of its uses 'the seat of consciousness, thoughts, volitions, and feelings' and quotes Mill as saying 'Mind is the mysterious something which feels and thinks'. In academic circles it has become unfashionable to use the term 'soul'. Many substitute words are used in order to avoid this word while more-or-less saying the same, although referring to a non-corporeal substance or thing within the human body is a contradiction in terms. By means of such words one simply refers to specific functions of the human organism.

Thus, one of the functions of the term 'thinking' is that of referring to the human capacity for putting through their paces symbols anticipating a sequence of possible future actions without performing any action. There is nothing to be gained but confusion for a type of science which tries to hide what cannot be hidden. Altogether, reason, mind and other substitute terms for soul are references to a very high integration level of humans and especially to their capacity for steering conduct by means of foresight of its possible consequences over a fairly long sequence of steps. They are not entities of their own, but functions bound to organs. It may be convenient to speak of them as entities in their own right, but the traditional use of familiar fictional symbols such as reason or mind can do with an occasional shake-up. One might just as well speak of a non-factual fact, an insubstantial substance. The many-levelled set of functions reaches from the level figuratively represented as consciousness which flexibly mediates between a person's changing purpose and the rush of the changing world in which a person is placed and goes down to the level of the more automatic, hence less flexible levels of drives and drive-control which Freud, also using a reifying noun, called the unconscious.

A brief example may help to illustrate the fact that what we call mind is a structure of cerebral functions at more than one level, often represented as thought. It is not easy to catch oneself thinking. But if one does, one discovers soon enough below the level of step-by-step thinking in terms of a public language, forms of abbreviated thinking. By way of experiment some intermediary stations are skipped in the onrush of thought and people have difficulties in translating the rush of telescoped reasoning into the step-by-step language required for communication. The telescoped manner of putting linguistic symbols through their paces is often linked to thinking in terms of images. But that must be enough here. There is much spadework to be done in order to clarify the use of language symbols not only as means of communication but also as means of orientation in the form of knowledge and reasoning and their links to the complex undergrowth of pre-language drives and fantasies. In this context one can limit oneself to the removal of the conceptual barriers which today tend to set apart reasoning, knowing and communicating by means of a language. To put it as unequivocally as possible, human beings without language would also be human beings without knowledge and reason. Language, the medium which ensures that a human being can communicate and effectively act with members of his group, is indispensable for the full development of a human being capable of using knowledge and reasoning in the form of linguistic symbols as a means of orientation. They all are human functions directed from one person to others. They are made possible and in turn make possible the specific way in which human beings live together as groups.

Without doubt languages break up this world into little pieces. Dictionaries, for instance, may assemble all words of a language and present them in alphabetical order. But one could advance the exploration of languages only very little if one proceeded in the manner of classical physics by measuring isolated words. Sound-patterns socially established as symbols of events carry their message clearly from sender to receiver only if they form part of a composition of symbols such as sentences or if their symbol content is defined by the context as in the case of exclamations like 'Hello' or 'Good God'. A language is not simply a quarry from which a given speaker selects specific sound-symbols as the occasion demands, it also provides models of the composition of sound-symbols. If offers a separate name, a separate symbol for every experience within the reach of a group; it offers at the same time models of their relationship. Explanations in terms of spirit agents or causal agents are obvious examples. To some extent, therefore, a given language and particularly the mother tongue, pre-empts an individual's thinking. But it is not impossible, within limits, to cut oneself loose from categories implicit in one's languages, as this paper may show. The present tendency to treat knowledge, language and thought as independent, perhaps even as separately existing items without bothering much about their relationship, can itself serve as example. In traditional language one might say, it is symptomatic of an imbalance in the relationship between analysis and synthesis in favour of the former. To correct this imbalance is one of the aims of a theory of symbols. It would lead too far here to indicate in greater detail the complex relationship between analysis and synthesis. It must be enough to remain within the confines of this example and to indicate briefly that all three activities or products of people refer to perspectives of symbols: knowledge mainly to the function of symbols as means of orientation, language mainly to their function as means of communication, thought mainly to their function as means of exploration, usually at a high level of synthesis and without any action at a lower level.

All three are concerned with the manipulation of learned and stored memory images. I have referred before to the fact that one need not always set out item by item when mobilizing symbols of memory images for reflection in the same way in which they have to be set out in a considered language communication with others. They can be telescoped. Items of memory images which are indispensable if the manipulation of symbols has the function of a verbal communication may be omitted if symbols are put through their paces for the purposes of reflection. Memory images can be manipulated at different levels of synthesis. Take as a simplified example the case of strangers asking you for the best way to the central station. You have a perfectly clear memory image of the whole area through which the strangers have to pass. But now you have to verbalize your memory image in order to communicate it to these strangers, and at the same time to select for them the most favourable route, for they are in a hurry and could easily miss their train. So you begin to verbalize the image: Go straight on in my direction till you come to the third corner on the right hand side. There is a Chinese restaurant and the road you should take is called Barbecue Street. Cross to the other side till you come to a big square. . . . You find that you have forgotten the name of the square. But your memory image of the strangers' road to the station is perfectly clear, so you give them a brief roundabout description and send them hopefully on their way.

Thus, the symbols with which I am concerned here can be stored in memory and recalled as the occasion demands. They may be dormant memory images, may become active as pieces of knowledge guiding conduct and sentiment and then get dormant again. But the symbols explored here are memory images of a specific kind. They can be connected with the sound-patterns of a specific language. In a word, they are communicable. I am not concerned here, or am concerned only marginally, with memory images of the private type scarcely connected with the sound-patterns of given language. Both can have the character of fantasies, but in one case they are private fantasies and the other public or social fantasies shared by different individuals. There are no hard or fast boundaries between the two types of memory images. References to the distinction may make it easier to perceive the limits and the focus of this enquiry. It may make it easier to understand the fact that both the use of language as symbol of something which really exists and its use as symbol of something which does not exist are characteristic of the equipment which distinguishes the human species from all others by comparison with the use of social symbols in a manner which is judged to be highly reality-congruent and thus classified as rational or reasonable. Their use as representatives of fantasies is still greatly underrated as a distinctly human characteristic.

Symbols of fantasies are often regarded as not of the intellect, but as irrational. Yet in actual fact the human ability to imagine things which do not exist, events which do not occur and to communicate about them by means of appropriate symbols has at best only traces of an equivalent in the animal world. It is not only the father and mother of art, it also was and still is indispensable for the survival of humanity once a species came into being which was biologically equipped for orientation and communication by means of learned knowledge. Its members would have been lost in a world which for the greater part they did not and could not know without the capacity for establishing and communicating about imaginary knowledge. They filled the gaps of their reality-congruent knowledge by means of fantasy knowledge. They never totally lacked reality-congruent knowledge. Their knowledge of details within the relatively narrow circuit of their life was usually extensive. But adequate knowledge of the wider connections affecting their life inevitably escaped them. It required many thousands of years to grow to the present still very inadequate stage that was one strand of the social development made possible and perhaps necessary by the biological evolution of a species whose inborn means of orientation had weakened and softened, which had become dependent for its orientation and communication on a slowly growing fund of socially transmitted symbols. They could not know what caused a fire in brimstone from a nearby volcano. The knowledge that a fire-spitting dragon was sitting within the mountain or that a demon's smithy was situated there enabled them to take appropriate action in order to appease this spirit. Awareness of the fact that they did not and could not have a more reality-congruent knowledge of the nature of the volcano would have been tantamount to a confession of their own inability to influence the course of events. Myth directed their action.

Memory images can in a flash illuminate the position of an event in time- and space-relations with others. They have an integrating character. In a world in which other people exist besides oneself it is difficult to imagine that one can separate from the other functions of knowledge its language function or, more specifically, its function as means of communication. As far as one can see, there is no absolute structural break in the continuum leading from symbols or memory images with a high reality-congruence to symbols with a high fantasy content. I shall leave open for further exploration the question of the innateness of some symbols. There is some evidence which suggests that buildings with a large cupola arouse different feelings in human beings than a steeply rising minaret-like tower because the former are symbols of the female breast, the latter phallic symbols. This is not implausible, but there is not enough evidence for this view to carry conviction. It needs further scrutiny. The point I wish to make is that even if one discovers the biogenetic character of some symbols, no adequate conceptualization of such findings is possible if one represents biogenetic and sociogenetic symbols as antipodes. It represents the human existence more adequately if one conceptualizes the tissue of symbols of a specific language as a continuum in a condition of flux. Some of its sectors may or may not be biogenetically fixated while others are more certainly acquired through learning, can change in accordance with experience or the lack of it and are sociogenetic in origin. Acquisition of sound-patterns and the symbol patterns through learning is not confined to individuals seen singly. People can also learn or forget as groups. Once humanoid ancestors had reached a stage where orientation by means of knowledge had become the dominant means of orientation, they could have hardly survived the fuller awareness of what they did not know or, not to mince words, of the extent of their not-knowing. Nor, for that matter, could we.

Within its smaller scope their reality-congruent knowledge compared with ours was in many cases more detailed. But the scope within which earlier stage societies knew more details was and, in any given case still is, by comparison, narrow. As they could no longer orientate themselves without knowledge, fantasy knowledge, magic and myth, while often misleading them, also had for them a high survival value. Take the sun as an example. It has only been in the twentieth century that humanity reached a stage in the development of scientific knowledge which enabled scientists to present a reasonably realistic theoretical picture of the sun. They were able to work out a model of the evolution of stars such as the sun which showed how they came into being, how and why they developed, and how they decay and disintegrate. It may not be the last word about this type of star evolution, but in the form of this model the sound-symbol 'sun' had certainly reached a high level of reality-congruence. This level was unattainable as long as the science of physics had not produced a highly adequate theory of the nature of matter or energy. Our human ancestors, however, saw the sun rising in the east and setting in the west day by day for thousands of years without adequate means to know what it was.

It is likely that animals which orientate themselves primarily with the help of species-specific signals or, as we used to say, of instincts, do not ask questions such as 'what is the sun?' or 'who is that there up in the skies?'. Humans, however, were by nature equipped with the need to know. The sun played a part in their daily life. He was a possible object of communication. Human societies usually have a group-specific sound-symbol for the sun. During the earlier stages of knowledge development this symbol was primarily a symbol of that group's wishes and fears in relation to the sun. It gave group members the possibility to communicate with each other about the behaviour of the sun on the basis of a common background of knowledge about regularities and irregularities of the sun's behaviour. Above all it defined the sun's status and power among the beings of this world and thus helped to direct and to organize people's behaviour towards the sun and also towards each other. Without some knowledge of this kind, usually with prognostic implications, humans would be helpless: they would not know what to do and what not to do in the presence of the sun. Now humankind as a whole is slowly learning to give the sound-pattern 'sun' or its equivalent in other languages a more realistic, more scientific character.

In a society in which knowledge, like water, is easily accessible and relatively cheap, one may find it difficult to realize to the full the extent of the human dependence on knowledge for their survival. Understandably explorations of knowledge are preoccupied with the question of the rightness and wrongness of knowledge, with its cognitive value. By comparison the survival function of knowledge commands less attention. Yet, human beings are by nature organized in such a way that they cannot orientate themselves in their world and maintain their existence among other existences without acquiring through learning a comprehensive social fund of knowledge. At present one does perhaps not pay enough attention to the fact that the need to know is an aspect of the genetic constitution of humans. The human capacity for producing fantasies in answers to questions which present themselves has no less survival value than their capacity for discovering what used to be called the truth.

Their possible reality-congruence distinguishes these pre-verbal integrating memory images from fantasy-images such as those of day- or nightdreams, which appear to be symptoms of drive-control rather than of the orientation and control of a world in which one lives. It is a characteristic of fantasies that they are connections of experiences which one never has in reality except when asleep. In fact, fantasy is the twin brother of reason. Both are specifically human branches from the same stem. The stem is the ability of humans to form sound-patterns which for all members of a language group symbolically represent the same object of communication. By sending such socially standardized sound-patterns to each other and by receiving them in turn from each other, members of a language group are thus able to transfer to each other or perhaps from generation to generation large chunks of information which may or may not inform their behaviour individually. If it is more reality-congruent, we call it rational. If fantasy outweighs reality-congruence we may characterize it as irrational, wish- and fear-symbol or use one of many related terms. Both bear witness to the freedom humans have acquired by their nature to form memory images of everything within reach of their knowledge and cemented firmly with specific sound-patterns. According to present-day knowledge this freedom is virtually without limits.

Yet every individual language and thus the society whose language it is, sets limits to what, at a given stage, its individual members can communicate to each other, store in memory or otherwise do with it. Thus terms like rationality and irrationality are not simply, as they are often understood to be, polar opposites. The road to a finding that is reality-congruent may lead through a whole series of imaginative assumptions with the dominant character of fantasies. Fantasies can be milestones. Scrutiny of the evidence suggests that there are many blends and degrees of rationality and irrationality, of reality-congruence and fantasy-content of symbols. A simple polar pattern impoverishes communication.

Moreover, the emergence of a reality-congruent discovery from a series of experimental fantasies, its emergence from a process, helps to clarify the nature of reality-congruence of symbols as a process. It emerges that the dichotomies with which we try to master the problem of reality-congruence of symbols is a simplification; it does not do justice to the shades and degrees of the approximation to a genuine discovery. It impoverishes our imagination by encloistering it into the dualities of right and wrong, true and false and others of its kind. Let us use as the basic point of departure the conception of an imaginative and innovatory idea on the one hand, and its reality-testing on the other hand. Both are indispensable.

Occasionally one may come across the suggestion that any imaginative idea, any fantasy can serve as starting point for a genuine theory, but that is misleading. It is the reality-testing of fantasies which shows whether or not one has hit upon a promising track. It is rare that a new symbolic representation is at its first conception a full hit, fully reality-congruent. It may be fully contradicted by one's tests and in that case it may probably be wiser to abandon the track. But it may also be partly confirmed and partly rejected by the test. We are ill equipped with firm conceptions for such blends between fantasies and reality-congruent symbolic representations. Yet halfway representations of this kind can be encountered in any scientific literature frequently enough. What is to be done in such cases? The flaw may be damaging enough to abandon the track, or it may be small enough that I can get it out of the way. May the next person improve on the symbol web I have presented. Perhaps we should search with greater deliberation for symbolic determinations of halfway houses between fantasy and reality-congruence.

Take as an example the symbol theory itself. In my own view it represents a great advance compared with traditional representations such as abstraction or generalization. Moreover, it helps to unify theories of what are usually classified as separate and even as independent areas of the human existence such as language, knowledge and thought. But by doing this it opens up for further investigation problems which were at best vaguely and marginally asked and with which so far one could not come to grips firmly, such as the question of the relationship between speaking and thinking. I have opened the problem by referring to the telescoping of spoken or written language by the use of symbols in those operations we call thinking, but much work remains to be done before the relationship between the handling of symbols in full dress which we call speaking and the handling of symbols in thought operations can be regarded as fully clarified.

Moreover, the term reality in phrases such as reality-congruence presents problems which remain hidden or distorted if one tries to approach them without a process-sociological perspective. The development of reality-congruent knowledge, especially its ascendancy in the balance with fantasy knowledge in the form of the natural sciences, is itself a co-determinant of what people at a given stage perceive as reality. Thus, for instance, Newton's reality was more limited than Einstein's because the social fund of reality-congruent knowledge at Newton's time was more limited than it was in the time of Einstein. One might suggest that in relation to the physical universe as it was known in the lifetime of Newton his laws can retain their reality-congruence and thus their cognitive value. It is only if they are perceived in relation to the reality-congruent knowledge of a later stage, especially that of Einstein, that the cognitive limitations of Newton's theories become apparent. As I have already indicated, the capacity for producing fantasy knowledge is as fundamental and distinct a human gift as the capacity for producing reality-congruent or, in other words, rational knowledge and thought. The failure to find in one's theoretical models of humankind a place for fantasies is one of the factors responsible for the failure to link theories of culture, and thus also of religion, to theories of other aspects of human beings and their various manifestations.

Whatever else they may be, operas and museums exhibiting paintings, poetry recitals and symphony concerts, they and other cultural manifestations are also forms of communal fantasies enacted publicly by human beings together. People live in groups. The enactment of private fantasies, by each person alone, can be dangerous not only for others, but also for oneself. But the need for the enactment of fantasies is a very basic and urgent human need. The ubiquity of games or other cultural activities and the refreshment, the pleasurable excitement, they can give to actors and spectators bears witness to the fact. This is said by the way. It may help to stimulate thought; it may underline the neglect of fantasy knowledge by comparison with rational knowledge. But in this context the social functions of culture are a sideline which may be pursued more fully elsewhere.

At the levels at which these functions are most closely directed towards the control of the social and natural world into which a person is placed, the kinship of language and thought becomes most directly apparent. The forms of thinking which one encounters there are often regarded as prototypical forms. Among them one often encountered activity is the experimental manipulation of sound-symbols representing possible courses of action, in anticipation of their performance in reality, in order to find out which of several possible courses of action is most likely to lead to the desired goal. While at other levels the structure formed by this set of controlling functions may be more akin to the flow of daydreaming, of pre-language imagery. At this level where control is directed towards other existences, thought is not easily recognizable as a flow of voicelessly-produced sound-symbols. It is, at this level, most easily convertible into spoken language, and spoken language most easily into the voiceless language of thought, although in that form it has often the character of a shorthand. It can be an abbreviated version of the audible use of language, but whether longhand or shorthand, audible or inaudible, language and thought are inseparable. Without learning a language, i.e. without learning to communicate with other human beings by means of sound-symbols, a person could not perform the kind of thinking which enables human beings to come to grips with the kind of problems that arise from everybody's co-existence with others, human or non-human.

Once more it may be easier to follow the line of thought if one ceases to treat the highly individualized modes of thinking which play a large part in more developed societies as a gift of human nature, and remembers that in earlier stage societies thinking in groups with the help of language exchanges often plays a larger part. The inclination to consider speaking and thinking as human activities which take place, as it were, in different compartments of a person and thus independently of each other, is at present certainly very strong. It is powerfully reinforced by a longstanding tradition which classifies thinking much more firmly than speaking as part of human nature and thus as unlearned, and in fact sees the capacity to think as the highest distinguishing mark of humans, and thus as the core of the human identity. The ability to use a language is more obviously acquired through learning and thus ranks lower in the implicit value scale, which gives pride of place to what is regarded as human nature and thus as unvarying and eternal. The intertwining of a natural growth process and a social learning process which plays a central part in the development of the human capacity to commu-nicate with each other by means of a language, is more difficult to understand. It is also more difficult to fit into the traditional value scale according to which unchanging eternals take pride of place over data in a process of change. Reason or mind perceived as part of human nature and thus as unlearned, is placed among the former and ranked accordingly, while language, which has to be learned and is subject to changes, according to the same value scale ranks much lower. Distinctly different positions on a value-scale which is widely considered as self-evident, are one of the major obstacles to the perception of factual links binding thought and language to each other.

Oddly enough, while the human faculties to which one refers as reason or mind are considered as part of human nature, they are also often enough perceived as the centre-piece of what is considered as non-nature in humans. One encounters here one of the symptoms of the confusion that frequently arises, if one tries to smuggle through one's arguments the undeclared luggage of a doctrinal value schema. Something similar may be said of what is traditionally called the laws of logic. They need not be mistaken for the science of formal logic, a quasi-mathematical form of scientific enquiry whose cognitive function and value is not in doubt. The traditional laws of logic are often seen as comparable to the laws of nature, if not actually as part of them. They too are used as evidence of the unvarying character of the human mind as proof of the fact that mind is a human universal working in the same way everywhere regardless of the changing conditions of language and of knowledge. They are for the greater part tautologies of little cognitive value, but they give support to the assumption that hidden within the human person, most likely within the brain, there exists a mysterious agency which functions according to its own laws, independently of anything human beings acquire through learning and thus of language or knowledge.

That must be enough in this context to indicate briefly some of the hurdles that stand in the way of a better understanding of the relationship between language and what is called mind, between speaking and thinking. The greatest of these obstacles evidently is represented by concepts such as reason or mind which make it appear that thinking is done not like speaking by human beings as such but by a special agency within them, which is independent of all other functions of a human person and follows laws of its own. So that no person can ever know what the world is really like without its intervention and, moreover, it is supposed to form part of the nature of humans, yet unlike other manifestations of nature is invisible and intangible. Many people must know that references to the human mind or to other agencies of this type are a form of philosophical make-believe, that thinking, like speaking and knowing, far from residing in splendid isolation within the human head, is one of many interdependent cerebral functions. Yet it is not often clearly said.

Linguistic usages such as that which makes everyone talk about 'the human mind', 'human reason', 'human rationality' may give the impression that all persons who use these words clearly know what they are talking about while in fact that is often not — one might even venture to say not often — the case. One encounters here an odd case of mental inertia. Custom invites us to engage in a little social game and cover it up with a conspiracy of silence. Let us all pretend that the human mind or reason is not less accessible through a scientific scrutiny than the human stomach and see what happens next. What happens in fact is, of course, that the unsolved problem which bothered us as long as we were conscious of it as an unsolved problem, stopped bothering us. It was simply swept under the carpet. We could forget about it simply by pretending that it had been solved. Expressions like reason, mind, rationality and so forth were all designed to cover up our little pretence. Like their common ancestor, the concept 'soul', they all pretended that humans possessed by virtue of their nature a special organ or faculty which had all the symbolic characteristics of a biological organ, substance or force, but which was insubstantial. No human being had ever seen it or otherwise examined its insubstantial substantiality. Yet many people were willing to commit themselves to very firm statements about the properties of this intangible organ. Whether they discussed it under the name 'soul' or under names like 'mind' or 'reason', its ontological status and its relationship to other more corporeal aspects of human beings never ceased to be problematic as long as human beings still found it in their heart to discuss such problems openly. Nor did they cease to be problematic when they largely stopped doing that. By treating as existing something that does not exist, learned people would do no harm with their intellectual games if, by doing this, they would not close the door to the investigation of problems, which at the stage at which we find ourselves are in need of closer scrutiny. The problem of the relationship between language and thought is a problem of this kind.

I am doing nothing more than opening a door which for some time has been locked and sealed rather firmly. I am doing that in this context because both speaking and thinking appear to me as ways of using sound-symbols. This basic similarity, perhaps identity, is, I believe, at the root of the possibility to convert speech into thought and thought into speech. The traditional human image associated with thought, and thus also with mind, is that of an isolated human individual. As one may have noticed I am no longer following that tradition. Communication in the form of human speech, communication by means of a language or, in other words, by means of socially standardized sound-symbols, presupposes as the normal form of living a life in groups. So does the activity we call thinking. It is perhaps useful to seek entry into the problems of the relationship between thinking and speaking at an earlier stage of development, at a stage where those who thought had not yet gained the characteristics of a specialized group; where groups who did were still identical with groups who thought; where, in other words, those who did also did their own thinking.

Perhaps one may do well if one takes one's first cues for the relationship of thinking and speaking from a hunting band rather than from the scholar's study. Their groups of scouts had advised the groups mainly engaged in hunting, virtually all the grown-up males, that a group of buffaloes in a fine condition was advancing towards the river about a day's journey to the west. There were other possible choices for the provision of meat food. Not only food choices determined the outcome. In all likelihood participation in the hunting entitled a person to participation in those aspects of the preparatory activities most closely related to what we might call thinking operations, to participation in the working out of a pre-paratory campaign plan. But in this case, too, aspects of the group's survival operation which we might call thinking had a much more pronounced interpersonal character than the standardized image of thinking operations which determines our use of the word thinking. In this case too, that humans are able to play with symbols of a future situation and to explore their suitability to one's own purposes symbolically has advanced so far beyond the animal level that wholly new forms of living together and of manipulating non-human nature have emerged from them. The buffalo hunters were capable of working out a detailed and precise plan of future action weeks or years ahead of its execution. The example may help towards a better understanding of the reason why the symbol emancipation, the emancipation of human action from the dominant bondage to here-and-now stimulus, is presented here as a major step and most certainly a very decisive step on humanity's road towards the position of the dominant animal species on earth.

Because people interested in enquiries of this kind usually live in highly differentiated and individualized societies, they are inclined to consider the highly individualized forms of thinking which are common in societies of this type as if they were the normal and thus also the natural forms of thinking of all human beings everywhere. Perhaps the time has come in which it can be accepted that this is an error. Thinking as well as speaking relies on socially standardized sound-symbols. Both are social activities. The nightmare idea that thinking exudes from an invisible autonomous agency such as reason or mind enclosed within the head of every human being, is not uncharacteristic of the self-image of people living in societies of this kind. The notion that the internal structure of this autonomous agency impedes the human capacity ever to know whether what they perceive is real or merely a reflection of the autonomous structure of that thing in their head, is a horror fantasy of highly individualized people. If nothing else, the rise of humanity to the status of the dominant species of living creatures on earth, contradicts the assumption of a fatal flaw in their natural equipment to orientate themselves in their world. The success of humanity in a very long struggle for survival rather suggests that they are by nature equipped with exceptionally efficient organs for orienting themselves realistically in their world. No structural impediment to their reality sense has yet come to light. As a precaution against misunderstandings perhaps one should add the obvious: the civilization of humanity itself is an on-going process and a possible aim of action. Nothing in present and past experiences justifies the assumption that the humanization of humanity is an impossible task, nor is there any good reason for the assumption that it is more likely than de-civilization. It is neither more, nor less likely. It is a useful and indeed an indispensable task to bring to light more factual knowledge of civilizing and de-civilizing processes and the conditions under which they become operative in relation to each other.

VI

Language, thought and knowledge are concepts broadly speaking at the same level of synthesis. Looking at the current use of these words one might come to the conclusion that they refer to different and separately existing groups of events, comparable to the different classes of animals to which one refers if one speaks of fish, insects and mammals. But that is not the case. Customs of research have made it possible that different groups of specialists may be concerned with the study of each of these items. There are theories of knowledge which pay scant attention to language and theories of language which have little to say about knowledge. Yet a language is undoubtedly part of a person's knowledge and a good deal of the knowledge which a person may learn has to be acquired by means of a language, even though the ratio of knowledge acquired with the help of communications in the form of sound-symbols and knowledge acquired without language communication may be different in different societies and in different branches of knowledge.

It is one of the oddities of mainstream theories of knowledge, of traditional epistemology, that most of them have little to say about the transmission of knowledge from person to person and almost nothing about the structural characteristics of knowledge which makes interpersonal and thus also intergenerational transmission of knowledge possible. Language communications play a major part in this transmission. The ratio of verbal and non-verbal transmission of knowledge may vary. But the wholly wordless transmission of knowledge is comparatively rare. That the major and, in some respects the indispensable part, played by language in the interpersonal transmission of knowledge finds relatively little attention in traditional theories of knowledge is no accident. It is due to the human image underlying these theories and to the problems which, in accordance with this image, appear as theoretically relevant and which do not. Essentially these theories are concerned with totally independent and isolated individuals. An imaginary person of this kind is perceived as the subject of knowledge. Hence interpersonal communication by means of a language, if it finds any attention at all, can play at the most a marginal part in these theories.

Also, the knowledge regarded as relevant in these theories is almost exclusively scientific knowledge and often enough only the knowledge of physicists. The argument seems to be that they alone produce knowledge that is valid or 'true'. The basic human image of an isolated individual as the subject of knowledge and of physics as the exemplary, the model-setting science, results in a limited and oddly foreshortened view of which knowledge in terms of these theories is relevant and of which is not. Individual great scientists hold the centre of the stage. If the transmission and growth of knowledge is considered at all, attention is focused on the sequence of outstanding individuals. How did science get from Newton to

Einstein is a model-problem. As a rule, pre-scientific knowledge is disregarded even if it is obviously valid or true knowledge, such as that of the stone and metal workers or the early agriculturalists of prehistoric times.

The field of knowledge regarded in these theories as relevant is, in other words, largely self-centred. The frame of reference is not humanity. The question is not how humans universally acquire knowledge. The prototype question of these theories is how a scientist acquires knowledge of nature on his or her own, independently of any knowledge she or he may have acquired from others. Given this individual-centred framework it is understandable that the relationship between language and knowledge, between the means of inter-personal human communication and the means of human orientation, has little relevance. So has the question of the distinguishing characteristics of human knowledge. The theories of knowledge which, broadly speaking, since Descartes have dominated the field, have the appearance of universal theories covering the whole field of human knowledge, but they are in fact almost exclusively concerned with a narrowly selected type of knowledge. They see this limited field in the light of a human image which makes people appear as individuals without society, as people who can say I and not We or You, as humans of the *homo clausus* type. Artifices of this kind make it possible to keep theories of knowledge, of language, and of thought, as it were, in separate compartments. As a result, they have usually little to say with regard to the ontological status of knowledge, to the question as to what knowledge actually is. In the manner of the time one might expect a sharply polarized answer to this question, an answer using alternative terms such as: nature or society, materialism or idealism. A closer look at the nature of language, however, has already shown that in certain respects human beings cannot be conceptually divided and polarized in this manner. Language, it emerged, is one of the missing links between nature and society or culture. Humans, one might say, are by nature made for culture and society. Knowledge, closely related to language communication, is another example of this kind.

Traditionally, theories of knowledge are fashioned without regard either for the physical aspects of knowledge in the form of the sound-patterns of a language and the cerebral memory images, or of the social standardization of sound-patterns which enables them to function as symbols of specific objects of communication, or in other words as concepts. What has been said before about language

No need to make a dishuttle between spirit + nature.

may make it easier to understand that knowledge, too, cannot be fitted into such conventional classificatory polarizations. Concepts such as cerebral memory images sit askance in relation to both matter and idea, materialism and idealism. The same can be said of the concept of sound-patterns socially standardized as symbols, known as such by speakers of the same language and thus capable of serving as messengers between the mouth of one person and the ears of others. No doubt speakers of the same language can sharply disagree in their views expressed in that language. But attention to their disagreements, ideological or otherwise, must not be allowed to obscure the awareness of how much knowledge they have in common as speakers of the same language. One can disagree about the nature and universality of cause and effect relationships, but one must have in common a concept of causal relationships in the sense which this term assumed with the rise of the natural sciences. In fact, like language, knowledge too is made possible by the intertwining of natural and social processes. It is difficult to imagine a knowledge transmission without language communication and without knowledge transmission from one generation to another a human baby could not grow into a fully developed human being. In actual fact learning to speak, i.e. learning a language, is in itself a form of acquiring knowledge.

With all this one does not establish yet another existential divide such as that between matter and spirit or nature and culture. Human society is a level of nature. Astronomers, biologists and perhaps some other specialized scientists rightly make and test guesses at the coincidence of circumstances which brought about this astonishing event, the evolution of human societies within this sun system. We still lack concepts capable of representing adequately the singularity of this event. By and large one is still inclined to bypass changes in the astronomical position of the earth and of the biological species living there. In some respects human societies are distinctly different from other animal societies. I have mentioned already the changeability of human as distinct from the rigidity of animal communications. The growth potential of human knowledge belongs to this category. So does the possibility to transmit new knowledge to the following generations. The possibility to form new concepts is made possible by the infinite variability of sound combinations which the human vocal apparatus can produce.

As I have already pointed out, in the case of non-humans social change is bound up with gene change, with biological change.

Human societies can very radically change without gene change. The same can be said of specific aspects and manifestations of human beings. Take language as an example. It is quite usual to speak of animal languages. But in fact no other animal species has the biological means which are necessary for communication by means of learned languages which are not species-specific but group-specific. But although human beings are in some respects quite different from other animals, they also retain many animal characteristics: they eat, digest and reproduce themselves like animals.

However, their differences from other animals are inadequately conceptualized if they are simply seen as differences of species. The differences between humans and apes are in some respects those between different species, in others they are much greater. They may approach in their character in magnitude differences between different orders of species. The ability to communicate by means of learned symbols is an example. It is almost totally lacking in apes. One of the reasons why we cannot come to terms with the problem of the ontological status of human beings in relation to that of animals is the inadequacy of the concepts at present available for this task. The frequency with which one uses in this context expressions which suggest that the singularity of humans is due to the possession of an invisible and intangible organ or substance which animals lack no doubt is also due to a certain intellectual inertia. Such concepts are easy to handle and almost everyone one meets uses them with some tacit mental reservation. The groundwork of concepts with which one works in the human sciences looks very solid and firm. But its vast underground edifice, nowadays, is rarely subject to a serious inspection. Much is taken for granted. If these fundaments ever did cohere, they hardly do so now.

Eventually one may be able to narrow the gaps of knowledge. One may get nearer towards a frame of reference showing how, why, where and when pre-human ancestors of ours transformed themselves into human ancestors and set in motion a self-civilizing process of humanity. Good luck may lead people to discoveries about the time when the great procession passed by. At present too little is known of all this to make intelligent guesses worth one's while.

What emerges quite clearly even from such a short and preliminary preview is the direction of changes in the groundwork of problems which are likely to make this work more promising and productive than it could be as long as a decaying immobilist tradition had a strong hold on it. There is a very obvious need for re-formulating and re-thinking. If that is done a basic pattern of change begins to emerge. Questions might be directed more consistently towards interlocking processes of long duration. The fact that until now the singularity of the dominant human means of communication and orientation has all but escaped detection may serve as a warning signal.

It is not difficult to recognize that humans are biologically equipped for two different types of communication, for communication by means of species-specific pre-language signals such as laughter and by means of group-specific languages. Then groups equipped for both techniques probably earned the reward by surviving in greater numbers. When the situation became stabilized again groups biologically equipped for both techniques, but with the accent on language communication, had become the prototype groups of further development. But specific forms of the older communication technique did not simply disappear; some of them became embodied in the now hominid prototype and adjusted to it.

Human beings are still equipped with an automatic device which makes them cry out loudly if they are in pain, thus communicating their distress to their fellows. The baby's automatic smile if it sees, or dreams of the mother, is also a heritage of the older type. There are other examples. They raise many questions. How are automatisms such as these selected for staying in, or for disappearing from, the prototype programme at a new level of development? How are the nervous pathways needed for nerve connections for a new type established? Moreover, there are likely to be many cases in which the integration of a new reaction path in the hereditary reaction programmes of a group approaches or even surpasses the level of complexity of the research language which is used to investigate this integration.

Once more a simple example may help. If a new reaction pattern is integrated into, or alternatively rejected from, the new prototypical programme of a group of mammalian animals, we may be inclined to conceptualize this innovation pattern in the form of a conceptual dualism, integration or rejection. There may be not only two, but six or even twenty alternatives. Take the example of smiling. People who are used to language communication may not immediately recognize that smiling too is a form of communication. Yet, that is what it is. In this case it is not the vocal apparatus but the face which serves as sender of messages from person to person. A smile on a person's face is in the first place a signal, a signal of the sender's well-being and friendly feelings towards the recipient of the message. One can perhaps assume that the ancestral forms of the smile of adults were less variable than they are in the only surviving type of hominids. Like many other more animalic communications the smile still is genetically pre-determined and bound to the situation here and now. However, in the case of human adults smiling shows very graphically how inadequate is the customary conceptual dichotomy in acquired and innate forms of behaviour by comparison with the observable evidence.

At a guess one might say that smiling is an ancient bio- and socio-genetic signal at an earlier stage largely under pre-cortical control which in the course of the change towards greater cerebral domination has come to some extent under cortical control. The baby smile is still largely spontaneous and automatic, a form of behaviour dependent on the condition of the whole organism and evidently not yet under cortical control. The smile of the salesperson welcoming you in a store is wholly 'put on'; the re-patterning of face muscles in the form of a smile which is among humans all over the earth innately recognizable as a signal of peaceful and friendly intentions, is in this case deliberately produced quite independently of the actual feelings of the salesperson. Between the baby's spontaneous smile that cannot lie and a person's deliberate production of a smile regardless of their feelings one may detect numerous intermediary forms. Adults can still spontaneously smile e.g. at the antics of a small child. But they can also suppress a rising smile if they find it inopportune. Members of different nations may react with a smile on different occasions in accordance with differences in their national code of conduct. These variations appear to indicate different blends of cortical and pre-cortical control of smiling conduct. Altogether the closer inspection of this particular form of human behaviour may help towards a better understanding of the fact that all forms of human conduct can be located on the map of the human organism or, in other words, located somewhere in time and space. That can be said not only of pre-verbal but also of verbal communications, it can be said of thought and knowledge. They all have a position in time and space.

This example may serve as a reminder that we are in these matters in a very early phase of our research. In the human sciences research in problems of biological evolution can easily have the air of a scientific doctrine which is well established and yet slightly antiquated. In their popularized form theories of evolution are certainly often gross simplifications. Some people appear to believe that the process of evolution runs its course with an automatic necessity; they assume for instance that the process of evolution must necessarily result in the emergence of a species of super-humans from the present species of humans. Relatively little attention is paid to the fact that the rise of humanity to a dominant position in relation to many other species has greatly affected the struggle for survival among them. In actual fact some species survive, some have perished as a result of human actions. The modification which the theory of evolution requires as a result of the ascent of humanity to a hegemonial position in wide tracts of the sphere of the universe within which animals and plants can live, does not often find the attention it deserves. The theory of evolution, far from being antiquated, is in its present condition most probably in one of the early stages of its career.

The same can be said of many other attempts of theoretical models of long-term processes and at a very high level of synthesis. Hegel's attempt at a synthesis of the development of ideas in the European context, Comte's model of the sequence of stages in the development of knowledge are characteristic examples. From a distance one can see more clearly that these attempts at a synthesis of the long-term development of knowledge were made as it were prematurely. They were made at a time at which the empirical evidence and the conceptual equipment available for the building of overall models of the long-term process of human knowledge were still rather inadequate for such a task. A good deal of inspired guesswork went into the making of these early models of synthesis. For centuries to come the work of these two men often served as deterrent examples indicating that in the field of knowledge attempts at a synthesis of long- term processes are bound to fail.

The experience is instructive. By turning away from the dynamics of the long-term development of knowledge one reinforces the tendency to treat knowledge as if it were a stationary object of the natural sciences, so the groundwork of our overall picture looks like a medley of unconnected bits and pieces. There is nature, there is culture, there is knowledge, scientific or otherwise, there are politics, economics and the all-embracing symbols of language, but how they all cohere with each other is a question that is rarely asked and hardly ever answered. Yet there can be no doubt that inescapable as this jumble of unconnected symbols may appear, in reality the processes to which these symbols refer are connected with each other and often enough intertwine. Nature and culture are a telling example. At present these concepts are formed as if they referred to totally independent segments of the world in which humans live. Often enough they are used as if they referred to polar antipodes, to two antagonistic spheres of our life. In the same way knowledge is often discussed as if its mode of existence were that of a disembodied entity and in this case too more often than not the biological organization of humans and their knowledge are symbolically represented as antagonists. Yet it is the organic structure of human beings which makes knowledge possible just as it makes possible communication through language and thus the transmission of knowledge from generation to generation.

Like apes and elephants human beings can acquire a good deal of knowledge through individual experience. But in each of these cases the scope of knowledge which can be acquired through individual experience without the use of words is exceedingly narrow. Acquisition of a language in fact gives an individual human being access to a social pool of knowledge which merely in size is a multiple of what that person may learn from non-verbal personal experience alone. The pool of a language in fact contains the sediment of experiences made in the course of many generations by many different individuals and deposited there in a symbolic form. It not only colours all experiences made by single individuals themselves, it also enables them to draw on experiences and reflections of others. In short the knowledge upon which people act undergoes an explosive expansion if through acquisition of a language they become connected with the knowledge pool of a society.

Whichever track one follows in such a hypothetical reconstruction of the past, in certain respects they all lead to the same conclusion: living together with each other while demanding specific curtailments of pleasure, offers to the human species survival benefits higher perhaps than to any other species precisely because with the help of their languages, their complexes of socially standardized symbols, individuals of a later generation can make use of the results of experiences of earlier generations. They can also forget them. This ability to draw on knowledge resulting from the experiences and reflections of previous generations greatly enhances the survival value which living together with others or, in other words of society, has for its individual members. The communal growth process of knowledge with its balances between absorbing and forgetting knowledge made over many generations is a field not yet sufficiently studied. At a guess one might say that only those of our forefathers survived the merciless test of the primal survival struggles who fitted the requirements of a life together with each other. At present modes of thinking have gained the upperhand which make it appear that living together in societies means living in opposition to human nature. In point of fact all the signposts one comes across in such a hypothetical reconstruction of the past point in the opposite direction. They indicate that humans are by their nature made for a life with each other, a life which, seen realistically, includes inter-personal and inter-group struggles and their management.

But the signposts seem to point in the opposite direction, at least partly, because the traditional form of analysis and the symbol formation following from it compel us to perceive as separately existing manifestations of humankind what are in fact different functions and different perspectives of the same manifestation. They compel us to reflect upon and to speak of language as if it were an object apart from knowledge, of knowledge as if it were an object set apart from thought, of thought as if it were an object set apart from language and so forth. We are inclined to block out a perspective of the signposts by representing as separately existing and perhaps as polar opposite aspects of humankind which are in fact substantially identical and functionally interdependent, such as human nature and human society, or language and knowledge.

No doubt the mother swallow can set an example for, and can coax from a distance with her voice, the hesitant fledgling on the verge of the first flight from the nest, but she has no means of transferring to her child the flying knowledge she has gained from experience. Apes as well as humans can gain knowledge by imita-tion. They can learn from examples. But, as I have indicated before, the scope of wholly wordlessly acquired knowledge is extremely limited. The uniqueness of the human neural and vocal organiza-tion, including the greatly extended human capacity for storing sound-patterns and thought-images in their memory, represents an organic basis for storing and for mobilizing knowledge, which is unequalled in the world we know. Given the intellectual climate of our time, it would not be surprising if the inclusion of biological aspects in any theory of language and of knowledge is classified as materialism. The observable evidence quite unequivocally steers exploration to the problem as to how a natural growth process and a social learning process intertwine. This question is obscured by the traditional custom of conceptualizing observations in terms of polar opposites. By conceptualizing problems such as this in terms of separately existing entities such as nature and culture one opens the cockpit for a struggle between materialists and idealists. In this case as in many others it is not the evidence itself which demands formulation of the problem in terms of an either-or, but the social tradition, the intellectual style of those who formulate problems in this way.

Take the customary classification of theories as either materialistic or idealistic. The human form of orientation with the help of knowledge, of communication with the help of a language, requires specific biological structures. Examples are the greatly extended memory tracts of the human species and the vocal apparatus apparently capable of producing an infinite variety of sound-patterns. Structures such as these, however, are hardly comparable with pieces of matter such as rocks or hydrogen atoms. As I have indicated before, these structures, far from being antagonistic to society can fulfil their function only if they are socially patterned. The integration of symbols of these structures into the theory of knowledge does not entail an intellectual reduction of ideas to matter. Nor is it compatible with the idealization of ideas. The symbolic representation of ideas as disembodied entities existing beyond time and space results in phantom theories without any cognitive value. It is a strange experience to live as it were in a period of transition from the rule of one paradigm in theories of knowledge to that of another. It may well represent the change to an era where familiar polarities such as that between materialism and idealism appear as irrelevant as the Medieval quarrel between nominalists and realists and where even in the field of the human sciences reality-congruence of knowledge gains precedence over ideological dogmatism.

The evolutionary stages through which the ancestors of present day humanity passed on the road from communication mainly through inborn signals to communication mainly through language, are still largely unknown. So is the bio-genesis of the use of socially standardized sound-patterns as symbols which could be understood by senders and receivers of a message within the same language group as symbols of the same object of communication. But the gap in our evolutionary knowledge does not prevent the possibility of saying very clearly what distinguishes animal from human communication, and what consequences this difference has or had for the development of humanity. In this context

I select for attention mainly two of these consequences.

Firstly, compared with human languages, the means of communication at the disposal of animals are relatively undifferentiated. One of the possible assumptions is that advances in differentiation and the corresponding advance in conceptual integration may have occurred in small stages mingling on occasions with explosive bursts of innovatory change in the same direction. Let us assume that in a field of primate groups with species-specific communications one group arose with some forms of more highly differentiated verbal communications, whose symbolic significance was only known to members of this group. The differentiation of this kind could not only result in a more differentiated cooperation of group members in the case of struggles with other groups of proto-humans or animals, but it also could strengthen the cohesion of such a group in action. Only members of this group knew the significance of this increment of differentiation in sound-patterns. Only they could act accordingly. In that way the learned increment of group-specific differentiation could have helped to increase the cohesion of a group. It increased their members' capacity to coordinate their activities. Added cohesion would have given many advantages to such a group, it could help to increase their success chances in hunting and inter-communal rivalries. A group might learn to vary the customary species-specific cries of fear and anger at the approach of an enemy according to the direction from which the enemy came, or according to the kind of enemy one might expect. In a word, greater variability of the means of communication offered a group evolutionary rewards.

Secondly, one of the most pronounced advantages of human language communication over animal communication, whether postural, vocal or whole-body communication, is the relatively high precision of the information communicated from person to person. Also, compared with pre-verbal exchanges, verbal communications can be more flexible, more closely adapted to a great variety of situations. One of the directions of the change from communication mainly by means of inborn signals to communication mainly by learned symbols is the direction towards greater distanciation from both the objects of communication and from its subjects, from the persons of the senders themselves. Animal communications represent to a very high extent information about its subject, about the condition of its producer. Humans have in no way lost this capacity. Yet representation of one's own condition by means of group-specific symbols presupposes a capacity for distancing the message both from its subject and its object which pre-human organisms lack. While requiring greater distanciation from subject and object than animal communications, verbal communications, thanks to their flexibility, can vary from greater subject-centredness to greater object-centredness and back again. They can be made to become more object-centred or more subject-centred, more detached or more involved. Take as an example the message 'we speak English'. It can be a highly detached and fact-oriented message. It can also be a highly involved rebuff of anyone who would dare to speak any other language. The message has its fact-related aspect which keeps at bay the influence upon its meaning of the sender's condition. At the same time, it can serve as a means of conveying to others the sender's condition. It is more object-centred than the miaowing of a cat, but it has also a limited scope for conveying to others the sender's condition. Even a rudimentary observation of language shows that a simple polarization such as that of 'subjective' or 'objective' or, for that matter, of 'subject' and 'object' will no longer do.

In fact, even the briefest examination of simple communications such as 'we speak English' can show the inadequacy of theories of knowledge which disregard the language aspect of knowledge. They are apt to imprison the imagination in an ontological landscape defined by the formula 'here am I — there is the world outside. How can I ever be sure that the pictures formed within me of the world without correspond to that world as it really is independently of myself?' The landscape changes if due consideration is given to the fact that the message is coded and that, however one may look at it, the code has developed over time in a particular social unit as its principal vehicle of communication, as its language. By handing over its language and knowledge resources to a rising generation it enables the young to become fully human. They are by nature designed for the absorption of symbols as means of communication and orientation. Their natural growth process prepares them for the integration of the social products. It is difficult to overlook the close interdependence of natural growth and social growth. Without it humans cannot develop adequate means of orientation and self-regulation. Yet in fact the intertwining of natural and social processes in the human case tends to be disregarded. Blockages of perception, whose reasons need not be explored here, tend to concentrate attention on cases where nature and society appear to stand in each other's way.

Lack of comprehension, of the nature and function of social symbols, the almost complete failure to provide an adequate symbol theory, are among the reasons for this gap in the present scientific equipment. However, attempts at filling the gap demand and may in turn stimulate far-reaching changes in one's basic assumptions and that is no easy task. The demand, for example, to break with the tradition which makes it appear that the scientific approach to problems of nature could be discovered at any time by people thrown back on their individual resources and in total independence of the development in their society and in humankind of a social pool of knowledge. This is one of the basic assumptions of mainstream philosophers in the line of Descartes, Kant and Popper. In the case of human beings, and in that case alone, the transmission of knowledge by means of social symbols enables later generations to build upon, to revise and enlarge the knowledge of earlier generations. Like language communication, inter-generational knowledge-growth is uniquely human. Though descended from, it is without precedent in, the animal world. I have already indicated that it goes hand in hand with other evolutionary innovations such as cerebral dominance and greatly enlarged, probably re-structured memory tracts where knowledge in the form of symbols can be stored.

But does not the language with which one has been brought up also act as a barrier blocking the access to new knowledge? Does not the inherited fund of knowledge interpose itself between people, the users of language, and the events of this world themselves? Are we not imprisoned behind the firm walls of inherited social symbols without which the world in which we live would remain unknown? One of the difficulties one encounters if one tries to find an answer to these questions is the almost automatic search for a spatial imagery facilitating comprehension. One may for instance be tempted to ask whether language and knowledge have the character of a window or a curtain. However, no spatial simile is of help here. Symbols are not pictures or mirrors of the world; they are neither windows nor curtains. They have not an imitative, pictorial, but a representational function. They represent objects of communication within a language community for no better reason than that of human nature which prepares the maturing child for impregnation with a communal language and that of social tradition which has made specific sound-patterns representative of specific objects of communication. The concept of meaning is a useful non-spatial way of approaching such problems. In the context of languages it stands for the symbol function of sound-patterns used as means of verbal communication. Awareness of the social character of languages, of their function as means of communication between a plurality of human beings is essential for the understanding of their symbolic function and thus for the understanding of the term 'meaning'. That words have a meaning can easily appear as a mystery if isolated individuals serve as the frame of reference. One would not need a language if one could exist in isolation. On that assumption it could appear inexplicable that the sound-patterns of a language symbolically represent the same data or, in other words, have the same meaning for different individuals. At the present stage it requires a spurt of self-distancing to realize that the point of departure for explorations of this kind is not oneself perceived as a person in isolation, but social formations, figurations formed by a plurality of human beings, by others as well as oneself. If that is understood, the nature of meaning ceases to be a mystery.

The sound-waves produced by the throat and the mouth of a person are destined for the ears of another person and are meaningless without someone else who can receive them. Everything which members of a language community may articulately experience and communicate to each other can be located in their language. It represents the entire world as it is experienced by them. Like time and space the tissue of symbols is all-embracing. As I have indicated, it may well be seen as another dimension. All that is known, is known by its name. The nameless occurrence is frightening. If the symbols of a language were not to some extent congruent with reality, with the data they represent, humans could not survive. Their orientation would be flawed, their communication full of misunderstandings. But the language can also contain common fallacies. Thus language can serve as a highly accurate representation of reality and as misrepresentations. One can try to uproot the latter although they have greatly diminished in some areas of our languages, especially in those representing the physical universe. But side by side with reality-congruent representations communal fantasies abound in languages past and present.

One cannot clarify the relationship between the representing sound-symbols and that which they represent without referring to the function which these symbols have for human beings. The traditional procedure, the description of the relationship between the sound-symbol 'table' and the table in our sitting-room as that between a general statement and a particular case is not wrong, but it is not enough. It does not help to clarify why generalizing versions of symbols may be of use to human beings. That comes to light only if attention is paid to the function of symbols. The general concept 'table' serves those who use it as a means of orientation. Activated from their memory store it helps people to diagnose particular objects, to determine their nature and their place among the manifold happenings of the universe. It also has a function as means of communication. It enables people to discuss with each other problems of specific objects, e.g. a particular table, even when they are not present here and now. General concepts form part of the common fund of a language. Even opponents may share them.

Recognition of the fact that one is for one's communication and orientation wholly dependent on communal symbols may elicit a claustrophobic feeling. Can one never break away from the orbit of symbols and come face to face with events which exist independently of them or of the world of humans generally? It may well be useful to distinguish more clearly between the mode of existence and the mode of representation of events. The fact that human beings depend for their orientation on the use of social symbols is perfectly compatible with the possibility to say that objects exist independently of human beings. It is probable that all language groups on earth have a sound-symbol of their own for what in its English version is known as the sun or the moon. This does not exclude the possibility to say that these heavenly bodies exist independently of human beings if that is what one wishes to say. The perception of sun and moon as gods or goddesses and for a time collective fantasies of this kind may have blocked the transformation of the terms 'sun' and 'moon' in the direction of greater reality-congruence. The example shows the extent to which the balance between fantasy- and reality-congruence in the meaning of words can change. Especially in the field of physical nature that balance has markedly changed in favour of the latter. Again the concept of the sun can serve as example. From being strongly fantasy-oriented it has become in course of time more and more reality-congruent. Thus the extent to which a language favours or blocks the access to events as they really are depends to a large extent on the stage of development of language and of knowledge at which a person is born.

The meaning of sound-patterns, their symbol content, can change. Evidence shows that over the generations defects of knowledge can be mended. Symbols are flexible. They can clearly represent objects as having an independent existence and structure of their own. If at a given time elements of a language distort reality, and there is no doubt that they can do this, the defect can be corrected. However, as changes of meaning as well as alterations or innovations of sound-patterns have to establish themselves in society at large, at any given time the scope for corrections is limited. This is one of the fundamental differences which distinguishes cognitive distortions and blockages produced by languages from the cognitive uncertainties supposedly due to transcendental units. The former are changeable, they are capable of correction. The latter are not; they are described as changeless, as eternally the same in all human beings and as totally impervious to new experiences. The basic doubt, the fundamental uncertainty as to whether human beings can ever acquire knowledge of the world as it really is which has become a *leit-motiv* of mainstream philosophy ever since it was formulated by Descartes, is based on a strange assumption which is rarely stated explicitly. It suggests that the cognitive functions of human beings developed initially on their own independently of a world to be recognized and that human beings having at first developed without object of cognition at some time, as it were by accident, entered an alien world. That, however, is a fable. Human beings have developed *within* a world. Their cognitive functions evolved in continuous contact with objects to be recognized. The symbol emancipation in the course of which socially acquired means of communication gained dominance over those which were genetically fixated enabled humans to adjust their judgement and their actions to an almost infinite variety of situations. Humans did not enter the world as aliens. Subject and object form part of the same world. The biologically predetermined propensity of humans to form sound-symbols of everything they experience and may wish to communicate to others bears witness to this fact. The categories they use at any given time in their communications with each other have developed and can develop further in their uninterrupted communication with the non-human world.

The assumed cognitive apparatus of humans, on the other hand, and the transcendental uncertainty connected with it in contrast to language and to knowledge, are not only presented as totally unchanging, but also as products of another world which have formed themselves in complete isolation from their objects. The philosophical antipodes subject and object and all the assumptions derived from them are wholly stationary. They are usually cast in a non-processual mould. If data observable only as changing, as happenings in a condition of flux, are presented in scientific symbolization as totally unalterable, as wholly non-processual, one is usually confronted with phantom problems which admit of no solution. One of them one encounters here. Patterns of language and of knowledge which individuals learn when young, which existed before they existed, do not hang in the air. They on their part must have been represented by individual persons. But one cannot stop here. Perhaps one can see the error of those who argue that a language is simply the sum total of the speech of individual speakers. Ideology in that case obscures the obvious fact that individuals are not free to utter whatever language sounds they like. In order to be understood they must use the same language as the fellow members of their group. Thus a language has a degree of autonomy in relation to any particular individual who speaks it. Yet it exists only if it is spoken by human individuals.

Thus one can easily be driven into a corner by the statement that all human individuals require by nature the patterning by a pre-existing fund of language and of knowledge, which in turn must have been the attainment of human individuals who had obsorbed the language and the knowledge of earlier generations. Both statements are valid: 'every individual learns a pre-existing social language' and 'a social language requires individual speakers'. If the problem — language prior to individuals, individuals prior to language — is cast in a stationary form it is insoluble. It invites a search for absolute beginnings where none can be found. But the enchainment of generations is a continuous process and in processes of this kind there are no absolute beginnings. Every human being learns a language from other individuals, but these other individuals also learned their language from other individuals. So where does the sequence begin? The need to find absolute beginnings is part of the social habitus of our age. As such it can change. It is early days for a change, but the need is likely to grow. Scanty as it is, the evidence points to a beginningless process with changing phases, but no absolute breaks. There is no reason to assume that our theoretical equipment cannot be fitted to the handling of processes of this kind. One is not eternally condemned to search for causes and beginnings where neither exist in reality. It is of great help to one's orientation if one fills the gaps of evidence hypothetically. The concept of a continuous evolutionary process is well suited to that task. At present we have no evidence and, as far as I know, not even a hypothesis as to how communication largely by means of genetically fixated signals changed into communication largely by learned symbols, but one can regard it as a very probable postulate *that* such a symbol emancipation occurred. The alternative is myth.

What kind of model emerges if the continuous process is represented as such? I have indicated before the need to distinguish between evolutionary and developmental processes. Here, at a new level of the cognitive spiral, one encounters an example. What emerges if one tries to fill the gaps hypothetically is in the first instance the by now familiar picture of an evolutionary process in the course of which the dominance of biologically inherited signals gave way to that of individually acquired social symbols as means of communication. These symbols were highly malleable and versatile. They were subject to changes as a result of changes in the fortune of a group or simply of coincidental occurrences. Thus the ascendance of symbol communication among our ancestors as a result of an evolutionary process gave rise to a process of change which was not evolutionary in character, which was not determined by gene-structures. It gave rise to a purely social, a developmental type of process.

The evolutionary process itself, that is the assumption, created conditions which set in motion developmental processes. There is no need to assume that in the ancestry of humanity evolution stopped when development set in. It may well be that groups in the ancestral line were subject to both types of change. Paleolithic people, for instance, not only underwent evolutionary changes, but very slowly they also improved their tools, which was a developmental change. So far nothing appears to be known about the capacity for communication by means of languages. However it was, this is an example of both types of change at work in groups of the same line.

In the case of the only surviving type of hominids changes of language and advances of knowledge are good examples of a purely developmental type of change. Whether humanity is still subject to evolutionary changes is difficult to say. In a continuous struggle for survival humans have gained supremacy over wide tracts of the animal world. In these tracts they have emerged as the winners of the struggle for survival. In their case one of the major levers of evolutionary change, the rivalry between almost equally powerful species, has almost ceased to be operative. On the other hand, developmental change has speeded up. In some respects the conditions under which, according to Darwin's classical theory, evolution of new species take place have radically changed. There are sectors of the animal world in which the unplanned process of evolution still continues as before. But there is one large sector where the free struggle for survival and the selection for survival of the fittest has almost come to an end. There, humanity has emerged as the fittest or, more correctly, as the most powerful type of living beings. If evolution continues there, it will be most likely a planned process, a planned evolution with unintended consequences. Humanity has gained the ascendancy over most of its potential rivals and enemies in the animal kingdom, though at the level of viruses and bacilli the struggle goes on. On other levels humans are largely in control. They have killed, imprisoned or confined to reserves other animal species and are just beginning to notice that rule over others entails some responsibility for them.

It is not an idle question in this context to ask how humanity managed to gain supremacy at these levels. Among the current answers the best known are individual-centred. One may refer to the superior intelligence of human beings, to the superiority of their reasoning power. Or else, one may refer to the tool-making capacity of human beings. But there is little doubt that in practice a major role in the power surplus they have gained over other species has been played by their faculty to transmit knowledge in the form of symbols from one generation to others and — in spite of set-backs — to the continuous growth of reality-congruent knowledge over the millennia made possible by its continuous inter-generational transmission.

The traditional type of developmental necessity had a strong naturalistic ring. It was almost taken for granted that a necessity of evolution such as that postulated by Darwin and his followers would continue forever. There were people who concluded from it that the theory of evolution implied a prediction according to which sooner or later the human species necessarily would be followed by another improved version just as hominids followed the apes. No such assumption is implied here. However, every social development is dependent on certain conditions. If these conditions change or dis-appear the consequent development is also likely to change or to come to an end. The emergence of humanity as the ruling group in wide areas of the animal world is an example. The strait-jacket necessity of the evolutionary sequence, which in previous centuries was almost taken for granted, conceals the complexity of the problem. It implies for instance a straight line development in the direction of progress. On closer inspection one usually finds that it refers to an advance in a highly specific area of society. It may well go hand-in-hand with what in retrospect may appear to be retrograde steps.

This is not the place for a fuller exposition of the problems of developmental progress and necessity. It must be enough to say explicitly what implicitly has been indicated again and again, that neither the concept of evolution nor that of development as used here implies a strait-jacket necessity or a uni-linear direction towards progress. What it does imply is an order according to which problems and problem solutions of a later stage presuppose a solution to problems of an earlier stage. The latter necessarily precedes the former, but the former do not necessarily follow the latter. To repeat the essential point: advances in knowledge of this type can make accessible to humanity's control problem areas inaccessible to it before. They can also act as a barrier to further extensions of knowledge. Perhaps it is worth indicating once more that this is the fundamental difference between the traditionally assumed transcendental units which give rise to the doubt as to whether human beings are ever able to acquire knowledge of the world as it is independently from them. These transcendental units are presented in a naturalistic manner as immovable and eternal. In contrast, symbols as intermediaries between subjects and objects are changeable. They can become more or less reality-congruent. In fact, some symbols of nature have become and can therefore become in future fully congruent with the reality they represent.

This changeability of languages, the fact that they may become more or less reality-congruent and altogether alter pattern and meaning is perfectly compatible with the fact that languages at all stages of development have certain functions in common. It may be enough to mention one of them. It graphically indicates the function of language as a means of communication between a plurality of human beings. I am referring to the function which in most modern European languages is represented by the series of personal pronouns. Together with the corresponding grammatical form of a verb this series serves as an indispensable means of orientation. It indicates to which person or group of persons a particular statement refers. It indicates whether it refers to the speaker or to a group to which the speaker belongs, whether it refers to a person who is present here and now, addressed by the speaker, or to a group to which the addressed person belongs and finally to a person not present here and now, to the third person or to a group which the absent person represents. The particular grammatical form which represents this function can vary. In Latin, for instance, the first person singular is symbolically represented by a form of the relevant verb itself. Ego, a separate word, is used only if one wishes to stress the fact that oneself is concerned with this or that activity. But whatever the particular grammatical form may be, it is used to represent this function; this itself, in one form or another is present in all known languages. Chaos would ensue if that were not the case. Compared with the spontaneous self-centredness of animal communications, the functions which personal pronouns fulfil are indicative of the greater self-distanciation and object-centredness which communication by means of a language demands of its speakers. In order to use in the appropriate manner a symbolic representation of one's own person, for instance the English personal pronouns 'you' and 'I', one must be able to look at oneself, as it were, from a certain distance.

Human languages of all kind compared with animal communications represent a higher level of object-centredness. This level of object-centredness imposes upon all languages certain common structural characteristics. The function fulfilled in some languages by personal pronouns is one of these characteristics. Hypotheses about the structure of languages are often presented without evolutionary comparisons. As long as one does not take account of the fact that the ability to communicate by means of a language is a stage in an evolutionary process, the common characteristics of languages cannot stand out clearly.

This is an example. Whether language communication emerged from pre-language communication in small steps, by means of a relatively rapid breakthrough or by means of both, its evolution formed a significant aspect of that of the only living human species. Although the details of this process are largely unknown, some of its results, some details of the change, stand out clearly enough. The greater detachment, the greater object-centredness of languages does not stand out clearly unless one compares language communication with animal communication. But there are other structural characteristics, whose function and significance may not come to light if one considers language simply as a symptom of a seemingly unvarying human mind, if one considers languages like many other characteristics of humans as results of an evolutionary process which may or may not continue.

Enhanced variability, flexibility and above all capacity for extension, are some of the characteristics which distinguish human language communication from animal communication. The latter is limited to functions closely related to the condition of the communicating subject and therefore relatively limited in scope. One of the innovatory bio-technical characteristics of languages is their elasticity, their almost infinite adaptability in the light of new social experiences. New social experiences, and among them new inventions and discoveries, sooner or later are symbolically represented in the language of a human group. It is a question which requires further research as to whether the unique human learning capacity, which enables them to make technical and organizational innovations, could have developed in the manner it did if human beings did not have the ability to converse with each other about novel experiences, to communicate with each other by representing sooner or later novel experiences symbolically by means of novel sound-patterns. A good deal of our evidence suggests that the ability to enlarge a given social fund of language and of knowledge by means of innovations, both of sound-patterns and of whatever they symbolically represent, is an indispensable pre-condition of scientific and technical innovations. Could human knowledge have been extended, as it was for example from the making of hunting-axes to that of computers, from the perception of the sun as a god or the vehicle of a god to that as a kind of helium burning furnace, without the enormously flexible and extensive character of the sound-pattern languages which came to serve humans as a means of communicating knowledge from person to person, and from generation to generation?

To be spoken, to use sound-patterns as symbols in communications between people, is in evolutionary terms certainly the primary function of language. But it is not the only function. I have already drawn attention to the fact that reading is a way of using the symbol functions without producing sound-patterns, and so is writing. In these cases the sensory patterns of sound have been replaced by the sensory patterns of vision. But there are uses of language entirely without any overt use of sensory patterns. The best known way of using language by manipulating symbols alone and by stripping them of any overt connection with sensory patterns, are certain forms of what we call thinking. In these cases, as far as one can see, the symbols retain the patterns they have received in connection with the language or the languages of the person who thinks. But the process of learning has made it possible to engage in a kind of silent speaking, in the manipulation of sound-symbols without uttering a sound, without any tangible sensory move whatsoever. But the silent language of thought can always be transformed into spoken language. However, there are other forms which consist, as it seems, of a manipulation of symbols without, or at the most with a rather tenuous connection with, the sentence-patterns of the spoken language. This type of symbol thinking may shade imperceptibly into the manipulation of non-verbal images mentioned before. Sentences may be reduced to key words which in turn can be blended with images. It is not always easy to transform thought or knowledge of this kind into spoken language, even though the patterning of symbols, as far as one can tell at this stage, remains largely identical with that which symbols receive in the language of a particular society. Closer and more detailed scrutiny is needed in order to find out how far even at this level differences of language and thus of social habitus make themselves felt. Do French-speaking people even at this layer use symbols differently from English-speaking people, and these differently from people whose mother tongue is Spanish or German? I am conscious that, with all this, I am raising questions rather than answering them. But questions too underline a point of significance in this context. Again one is being made aware that language, thought and knowledge cannot be treated as if they existed in separate compartments. They cannot be regarded as the subject matter of different theories. Specialization has outlived its usefulness. A unified theory is needed which embraces them all.

That language has its material aspects is easy to recognize. In order to fulfil its function as means of communication, it must not only be spoken; it must also be heard. The sound-patterns must travel from a person who sends a message to a person or persons who receive it. Once more one comes across the development of a group of humans with its specific language and with other habitus characteristics as a kind of social *a priori*. It exists prior to any experience of the newly-born human being and helps to fashion its faculty of speaking, thinking and knowing. This bio-social arrangement is the condition of continuity in the development of language, thought and knowledge. It accounts for the persistence with which in many cases distinguishing characteristics in the development of different societies or, as one often says, of different cultures, maintain themselves over the generations. However, for a better under-

standing of the consequential character of this arrangement it is not
enough to compare different human societies with each other. Its
full significance stands out clearly only if one ascends to a higher
level of synthesis, by comparing human societies with animal
societies. Members of the former communicate mainly by means of
a learned language; members of the latter remain in their means of
communication to a much larger extent bonded to forms which are
not acquired through communal and individual learning, but are
genetically predetermined forms of communication. A comparison
at this level makes it more clearly visible that language communication is one of the basic differentials of human society.

One of the most significant distinguishing characteristics of
human society is its capacity to change, to develop new forms, to
adapt itself to new conditions without any biological changes of the
human species. The structure of animal societies is species-specific;
the structure of a group of chimpanzees is always different in a
specific manner from that of a group of gorillas or gibbons. Wolves,
elephants or, for that matter, social insects, form almost unchanging
groups characteristic of their species. Their group-life has come into
being as part of the biological process we call evolution, that is as
part of the same process in the course of which the biological species
concerned emerged as such, and the timespan needed for such evolutionary changes is comparatively great, especially if one compares it
with developmental changes. If one thinks of the emergence of a
new species, one would probably be nearer the mark if one uses as a
temporal frame of reference millennia rather than centuries. Many
human societies have undergone vast changes within the short time-
span of the twentieth century, e.g. from tribes to states, from absolute monarchies to parliamentary republics. It took the Romans a
couple of centuries to develop from an Etruscan-ruled city-state and
an often embattled city-republic into the ruling group of a vast
empire. This type of social change without any demonstrable biological change of the species can, in terms of the concepts to be
used, be quite clearly distinguished as a social development, as an
unplanned change in one direction or another within one and the
same biological species, that of *homo sapiens*. It clearly differs from
the evolutionary changes which result in the emergence of a new biological species and which in the case of socially living animals
encompass the way these animals live together in groups.

For many thousands of years no doubt the tempo of social change
and of the extension of knowledge was very slow. It appears to grow

at an exponential rate. So did the fund of reality-congruent human knowledge. But the fact itself that it did increase over the generations was made possible by the evolutionary innovation of communication by means of human-made sound-patterns which served as symbols of anything that could become objects of communication in a particular society, and which had to be acquired through learning. Among them were, in all cases of which we have knowledge, symbols of the society where a particular language was spoken, a kind of collective self-image.

We do not know how the evolutionary change to communication mainly by means of socially standardized sound-patterns to be acquired by learning was achieved. But this gap in our evolutionary knowledge does not impair the possibility of recognizing that this novel technique of communication by means of a language, by means of socially standardized sound-symbols in its many-sided function as language, thought and knowledge, holds a key position in the transition. That is from animal societies whose structure is largely determined by the gene-structure of individuals, or in other words is species-specific, to human societies whose structure can undergo vast changes without any biological changes in the gene-structure of individuals and largely in connection with changes in group experiences, among them changes in power relations or in the social fund of knowledge.

One could argue that changes in the social fund of knowledge which could be transmitted from one generation to another might be handed on without the use of symbols by imitation alone. There can be no doubt that learning by means of imitation does play a part in the learning processes of individuals, and thus in the transmission of knowledge from one generation to another. It may well be that the often suggested imitative propensity of apes is the symptom of an increase in their learning potential. However, at the level of the still living species of apes, learning is still far from gaining the upperhand in the genetically determined balance between innately fixated and learned forms of steering activities. All-in-all, moreover, the scope of knowledge that can be transmitted through silent imitation and its correction without the use of language symbols, is small compared with that offered by the symbol technique of knowledge transmission. One need not forget the fact that wordless imitation can play a part in the human technique of knowledge transmission, but one can say that its potential as such is greatly surpassed by that of the symbol technique. There is virtually no limit in sight to the extension and changeability of sound-patterns standardized as knowledge.

Nor is the adaptability to greater reality-congruence of symbols curtailed by structures of its own deposited there by the nature of humans or in any other way pre-empting experience. If nothing else the growing reality-congruence of the human concepts now representing non-human nature can serve as an example of the ability of human-made symbols to develop in the direction of greater reality-congruence or the enlargement of the social fund of knowledge. It is also widely known that in all sections of humanity where a scientific type of knowledge of what we call nature has come to the fore this was preceded by a magico-mythical type. Its character as the realm of spirits with a greater or smaller power potential preceded the experience of nature as an evolving universe changing aimlessly but according to a built-in order.

The fact that the change from a mythical to a scientific image of nature is widely treated as commonplace knowledge and as such is taken for granted, often blocks the recognition of the fact that this is a telling example of one of the developmental directions in which sound-symbols can develop, an example of the development towards greater reality-congruence of symbols. Take as an example once more the changing image of the sun. That the sun has come to be regarded as a helium burning furnace, to express it in the language of lay people, may or may not prove to be the final stage of a cognitive process. It most certainly is a development in the direction of greater reality-congruence. The same can be said if one compares medieval bestiaries with a modern book about animals with many reproductions. In the former case one might find vivid descriptions of the unicorn and other animals, which we know to be products of human fantasy, which are presented as real. Mythical animals have largely disappeared from the popular books with pictures of animals of our own time.

There are numerous other examples illustrating the fact that the social fund of symbols can change from a condition in which the distinguishing line between fantasy knowledge and reality-congruent knowledge is uncertain and the balance between them is strongly tilted in favour of the former, to a condition in which the distinction between the fantasy content and the reality-congruence of symbols in the field of non-human nature is completely unambiguous. Here reality-congruent knowledge, in the balance between the two types, clearly has the upperhand. In this field it is clearly in the ascendency while in other fields, such as that of the knowledge of human societies fantasy knowledge, for example in the form of social ideals, still poses as reality-congruent knowledge. In these fields the distinction between fantasy and reality is blurred and the former clearly has the upperhand in the dominant forms of knowledge.

VII

Compared with traditional theories of knowledge which have dominated discussions from the seventeenth to the end of the twentieth centuries, the symbol theory of knowledge can itself serve as an example of a spurt from the greater pre-eminence of fantasies to a change in the balance towards greater reality-congruence. The expression reality-congruence is designed to help correct one of the weaknesses of traditional theories of knowledge — the tendency to treat knowledge as if it existed in a vacuum. As a rule these theories overspecialize knowledge. They treat its cognitive function, its function as means of orientation, as if it existed in isolation independently of all other functions, especially of its function as means of communication. The ontological status of knowledge, its place in the world and thus the relationship between knowledge, those who know and that which is known, remains unclear. The separation from language deprives knowledge of its anchorage in a multidimensional world. It simply appears as something in the mind of people. This status implicitly confirms the tacit assumption that knowledge, like language, is something immaterial, something that exists outside and independently of the material world, the world of time and space. However, it is a simple statement of fact that nothing can be said to exist which has not a place in that world. It is indicative of the phantom character of many current theories of language and of knowledge that their aspect as something in time and space finds scant attention in them. That everything which has a place in time and space also has a place in the symbol dimension is in no way incompatible with the fact that everything that has a place in the symbol dimension also has a place in space and time.

The tendency to speak of knowledge as if it existed beyond time and space goes hand-in-hand with others which suggest that it exists outside human beings. A whole vocabulary has been created to support this ethereal existence. Truth and validity are examples. They usually have a static character. They have been replaced here by process concepts. Sound-patterns standardized in a specific society as symbols of a particular item can be made more or, according to circumstances, less reality-congruent. The concept of truth has its function and its place in our vocabulary. At a law court a witness may be said to have told the truth. Of a schoolchild as of diplomats it can be said that they have told a lie. The antonym of the concept of truth is the concept of lie. The wounded man who after an earthquake told the hospital guards that he had been buried under the rubble for thirty-five days told them a lie in order to gain admission. But in a scientific context this pair of antonyms is less usable. One would strike a wrong note if one declared that the Alexandrian astronomer Ptolemy and his contemporaries told a lie while Copernicus told the truth, that Newton told a lie while Einstein discovered the truth. It is the rigidly static character of the concept 'truth' which contributes as much to its inadequacy as its moral undertones. Scientific work, however, proceeds step by step. It has the character of a process in the direction towards greater reality-congruence or towards a lower fantasy content of symbols on a variety of levels. Its statements can become more adequate as symbols of facts or less adequate. There are many shades and degrees of the congruence of sound-symbols with facts. That the sun is a heavenly body set into the skies by a deity in order to bring light into the days of humans is not a lie, but a fantasy and not even entirely wrong, for the sun is the source of daylight.

The uncertainty with regard to the ontological status of knowledge has been removed here by the reminder that knowledge is a sound-pattern that can be stored in the memory of a people, the socially established meaning of which can pass from a condition where fantasy prevails to another with a high level of reality-congruence. The central problem of knowledge and of cognition was and still remains the problem of the relationship between knowledge and its object, the facts represented by it. There was a time when people believed that knowledge inevitably distorts or blocks reality. If nothing else the advance of natural sciences and the technology connected with them contradicts this belief. Nothing is more characteristic of the basic uncertainty which clings to the use of the concept of knowledge and thus to all statements about its relationship to its objects, than the stigma attached to the use of the term reality. Philosophers are inclined to stigmatize as naive those who use this term in discussions about the nature of knowledge. How powerful the influence of transcendental philosophy is can be seen from the fact that people are afraid to use the term reality in discussions about knowledge lest they should be thought of as unprofessional, as not familiar with the doctrine that has come to be accepted as an axiom among the *cognoscenti* — the doctrine that knowledge inevitably distorts or conceals the real world. Errors, mistaken judgements are always possible. But in a period in which institutional scrutiny of the reality-congruence of claims to discovery, at least in some sciences, has been greatly perfected, the doctrine of knowledge as an eternal distortion or disguise of reality can be regarded as outdated. And indeed as long as the question: what is knowledge? is not asked and therefore not answered, how is it possible to answer reliably the question of whether and how far human knowledge corresponds to its object, to the reality which it represents.

The symbol theory, a brief outline of which is presented here, raises and answers the question: what *is* knowledge? It simply indicates what theories of knowledge lose through a sophisticated artifice. It restores to knowledge its linguistic character as messages from persons to persons in the form of more-or-less standardized sound-patterns. They serve humans in one form as means of communication, in others as means of orientation and, in the form of thinking, as a silent experimentation with possible solutions in order to find the most simple and best solution among them. On that basis one can say very clearly that knowledge bears no ontological similarity to its objects except if it becomes its own object. The crux of the matter is that traditional theories of knowledge usually fail to refer unambiguously to the substantive aspects of knowledge. They do not say clearly that knowledge consists of sound-patterns which are socially standardized as symbols of real events. I have consistently avoided in this context the use of the concept 'truth'. The term reality-congruence used instead also helps to clarify the relationship between the symbol and that which it symbolizes.

One sometimes encounters the tendency to explain that relationship as a kind of similarity. The symbol may be literally perceived as a picture or an image of that which it represents. However, in most cases, in all cases except in those in which symbols themselves are symbolically represented, symbols are totally unlike that which they symbolize. Knowledge of the sun is totally unlike the sun. It bears no resemblance to it. However, as a sound-pattern standardized among

NB] relativism is the human capacity to recognize
object fashioned in such a way as to deceive us?
112   THE SYMBOL THEORY

English-speaking people as a symbol of the sun, it may have a higher
fantasy content or a higher reality-congruence. In the course of
centuries it may move towards the former or towards the latter. An
image of the sun is associated with the sound-pattern 'sun'. In that
form it is stored in the memory of people who speak that language.
A scientific enquiry can eliminate fantasy elements from the object's
symbol and increase the symbol's object-congruity. In fact one of
the reasons why the concept reality-congruence has been introduced
here is the wish to avoid the picture- or mirror-imagery. The term
reality-congruence may draw attention to the greater or lesser con-
currence between objects and the knowledge about them. What can
be seen as knowledge, if its main function is as a means of orientation, can be seen as language if attention is focused on the message it
carries from person to person.

In that respect the symbol theory can perhaps help to bring to a
conclusion the long drawn-out controversy as to whether humans
can recognize objects as they really are or whether they are forever
prevented from finding out 'the truth' about the world in which they
live, and thus also about themselves, by the autonomous structure
of their cognitive faculty, by forms of thinking engraved in their
mind prior to any experience. This has been a strange quarrel, this
one about forms of thinking which exist in humans prior to any
experience of objects. For it implies, among other things, that
humans evolved initially without a world and thus without objects
they had to recognize, and that they entered the world, as it were, by
accident, as a kind of afterthought. In order to enter the spirit of
transcendentalism one has to consider seriously the possibility that
the human faculty of recognizing objects is by nature fashioned so
as to deceive us. Descartes very explicitly considered the question of
whether the world as we know it was not an illusion. It was certainly
more than a coincidence that a period at which in the form of
natural science a more reality-congruent type of knowledge gained
the ascendancy, also gave birth to the philosophical doubt as to
whether humans are able to gain any true knowledge of the world in
which they live; whether, in other words, the world as they
experience it is not simply an illusion. The species of creatures by
nature equipped with a defective faculty of cognition had, one might
venture to say, hardly a chance to survive in a world where many
animals, including beasts of prey, were by nature equipped with a
highly effective cognitive faculty.

The period in which Descartes raised this question was also the time in which the supremacy of the cognitive faculty of humans found expression in the growing human domination of non-human nature. This growing pacification of the animal world inhabited by humans is perhaps not entirely negligible as a symptom of the quality of human cognition. One may well ask why the human capacity for eliminating illusions, for giving reality-congruent knowledge the upper hand over fantasy-knowledge, in fields where humans themselves are the objects of enquiry, lags so much behind the development of their knowledge in the field of non-human nature. It is tempting to think that differentials of pacification have something to do with it.

However that may be, the basis of a discourse about the nature of human knowledge suggested here, as one may see, has changed. For one thing knowledge as perceived here is a process, the learning process of humankind, not the learning process of an individual person who supposedly acquires knowledge starting from scratch. That is a conception of knowledge more closely attuned to the evidence, although less closely to the tradition of knowledge theories. However great and innovatory the contributions may be which individual persons make to the standard knowledge of their time — and no one would wish to deny the part that extraordinary innovatory contributions of known individuals can play in the development of humankind's social fund of knowledge — it is the development of this social fund of knowledge which forms the spring and fountainhead of any individual contribution to knowledge. It is the reception into the publicly recognized stock of knowledge, often enough itself a lengthy process, which marks the transition from a private view which may or may not be the *idée fixe* of a single individual, to a contribution to humankind's mainstream of knowledge development.

Take as an example the concept of a sun-centred universe. It was known long before Copernicus gave it a form which could gain for it recognition among contemporaries and thus reception in the public fund of knowledge. It was known in Antiquity to Ptolemy of Alexandria among other people. He rejected it largely, it seems, because it was so obviously contradicted by the evidence of our senses. Conflicting views such as struggles for reception, form an integral part of humankind's knowledge process. One of the basic theses of this essay, the we-centredness of knowledge, the fact that knowledge has the character of messages from persons to persons, has to contend with similar difficulties. It collides with a deep-rooted ruling doctrine according to which knowledge is I-centred. The subject of knowledge can change from I, the first person *singularis*, to we, the first person *pluralis*. It is consistent with this change that knowledge is seen here as inseparable from language. The development of human knowledge as we know it would be impossible without the unique human capacity of transmitting knowledge in the form of language components from one generation to another. Whether it is an oral transmission or a book transmission, it is a fact that knowledge can be communicated in the form of a language from person to person, which makes the massive transmission of knowledge from one generation to another possible.

If one wishes one may distinguish between different levels of knowledge. But there is no language communication which has not the character and function of a transmission of knowledge. In that respect there is no essential difference between Einstein's famous formula symbolically identifying mass and energy, and the statement that the water in the kettle is boiling. Both have the character of sound-symbols and in both cases the sound-patterns carry knowledge from one person to another. Language and knowledge are not two different and separately existing data, but different functions of the same event sound-symbols, of sound-patterns symbolizing objects of communication. The concept of knowledge accentuates the fact that sound-symbols can be stored in the memory tracts of a person and in that case their vocal aspects may become temporarily silenced and inactive. But they are re-activated if the symbolized data stored in a person's memory are recollected from there and are once more prepared for communication as audible or visible symbols. This recognition of the substantial identity of language and knowledge makes it possible to remedy one of the major defects of traditional theories of knowledge. To say it once more, they do not explore the question of what knowledge actually is, its mode of existence. Its ontological status remains uncertain. Problems of knowledge are sometimes broached as if they were problems of nature, but knowledge is also often treated as an ingredient of culture and as wholly immaterial.

So far two major foci of deviation from traditional knowledge theory emerge. (1) As I have just said, knowledge, like language, is no longer seen here as an disembodied and ethereal idea of uncertain ontological status, in terms of its mode of existence. It is seen in the first instance as the actualization of a biological potential through a person's encounter with other persons. Like language, knowledge is seen as a web of symbols socially or, if one prefers, culturally, implanted in a physiological ground designed for this implantation. Without the reception of a stock of social knowledge human individuals cannot orient themselves adequately and thus cannot survive. Ontologically therefore knowledge, like language, belongs to the great tract of processes linking nature and culture or society. It is far from immaterial. Without social standardization of sound-patterns and the deposition of its symbol function in a person's memory tracts, the processes we summarily call knowledge would fail to materialize.

(2) The second major deviation from accepted doctrine about knowledge concerns the symbol character of knowledge. It helps to define more sharply what it is that is said to correspond to something else in statements such as 'this statement is true' or alternatively 'not true'. Traditionally one has to be satisfied that the discourse centres on the correspondence between ideas, concepts, theories or knowledge of a person called the subject, to facts of any kind, called objects. Here knowledge is not separated from the context of human communication. The question is whether and how far components of a language, socially standardized as symbols, correspond to that which they are intended to symbolize. An example is the expression 'human being'. It is a sound-pattern which symbolically represents you and me and every other member of the human species. This symbol can be sent in a message, as is the case here, from one person to another. Again, the question is whether and how far the standardized mainstream knowledge, which may be divided into humans as God's creations or as products of evolution, is reality-congruent, or how far it is fantasy allied with wishes and fears. This deviation, as one may see, implies a shifting of the focus from the individual knower as subject of knowledge to human groups and in the last resort humankind where the knowledge symbolically represented by specific sound-patterns or, as it is often expressed, their meaning, has come to develop its present standard shape.

Traditionally, the correspondence problem is set into a stationary frame of reference. Instead it is set here, in accordance with the evidence, into a processual framework. The great variability of sound-patterns and of the knowledge or information they are standardized to carry from person to person, makes it possible for whole groups of symbols to change over time from lesser to higher reality-congruence or alternatively from a lesser to a higher fantasy content. The peculiar character of the human vocal apparatus and its cortical connections also makes it possible to extend the sound-patterns of a language and to establish new sound-patterns as symbols of new discoveries, of new experiences generally, which demand communication. One may doubt that an extension of human knowledge would have been possible if the vocabulary of people, their equipment for producing sound combinations which could serve as carriers of messages concerning the novel experiences, had not been extensible as well.

The extension of human knowledge itself is well known enough. It is known that the growth of reality-congruent knowledge was relatively slow in the earlier stages, that it speeded up in course of time and is still accelerating. It is common knowledge that humans used for many thousands of years mainly weapons and tools with stone as their most durable material and that they slowly acquired the knowledge of handling metals as raw material for their weapons and tools. The rapid extension of human knowledge, especially in the field of non-human nature which one can observe in more recent times, is equally well known. The human groups which at a given stage pioneered innovations of knowledge, varied greatly; they were different in different stages of the development of knowledge. But the main innovations in knowledge, with great regularity, spread in course of time from the originating human groups to many others. The diffusion of new knowledge from certain centres to other groups used to be far slower than it is today, but it was a normal feature of the growth of human knowledge as far back as we can look.

All this is widely known. But it is known only at the empirical level. So far as traditional theories of knowledge are concerned, it has almost entirely remained outside their scope of consideration, even though it is obvious that everyone who uses the available fund of human knowledge or who contributes to its further extension, stands on the shoulders of largely anonymous predecessors, who individually or as groups made a lasting contribution to the growth of human knowledge. A deep-rooted epistemological tradition excludes this long process of knowledge growth from consideration at a theoretical level. One of the reasons for this blockage is most certainly the fact that the inclusion of the long-term growth process of knowledge into a theory of knowledge is not compatible with the basic assumptions underlying traditional theories of knowledge. It is not compatible for instance with the model of a subject-object relationship according to which the image of a subject is patterned on the assumption that individuals acquire knowledge on their own as totally independent subjects without any dependence on previous generations.

It is also often presumed that in a theory of knowledge only scientific and perhaps only physical knowledge is worth considering. Undoubtedly the transition to the type of enquiry which is now called scientific in the field of non-human nature can be considered as a breakthrough in the human quest for the extension of reality-congruent knowledge. But it is also beyond doubt that this breakthrough could not have been achieved without a long antecedent growth of pre-scientific knowledge in the direction of greater reality-congruence. Copernicus owed a lot to Ptolemy and other writers of Antiquity. The transition from a hunting and collecting stage to that of herding and agriculture also represented a step towards the extension of reality-congruent knowledge. Like the development of writing and reading, of the transmission of knowledge by means of visual symbols in addition to its transmission by means of aural symbols, the domestication of plants and animals was a step on the road which led from pre-scientific to scientific knowledge. Without these and other antecedent advances of knowledge, the breakthrough to the scientific way of extending the human fund of reality-congruent knowledge would hardly have been possible.

The traditional explanation of the coming of science as the quasi-accidental brainchild of a few exceptional individuals, can hardly do justice to the dependence of the pioneers of the scientific type of enquiry on antecedent advances in human knowledge and on the great body of reality-congruent knowledge about nature that had been growing up through the millennia prior to the emergence of reality-congruent knowledge in a scientific form. Without regard for the pre-scientific phases of the growth of the human knowledge of nature the breakthrough to the scientific phase cannot be adequately explained. A great deal of empirical research is needed in order to make these connections fully visible. But no less needed is a theoretical model of the growth of human knowledge that deviates from existing theories. The symbol theory of knowledge is an attempt in that direction, which represents knowledge as a long-term process, as sets of symbols in a condition of flux. They can move in one of two directions represented by a battery of criteria. Knowledge can advance or regress, expand or shrink. As indicated, it can become more reality-congruent, less fantasy laden or the reverse.

So far, then, humanity's knowledge of non-human nature, with many major and minor fluctuations, has steadily advanced in the direction of extension and greater realism. It can serve as a model of a long-term development in a specific direction and of the diachronic order characteristic of developments of this type of a one-after-another or sequential order. Any given later stage pre-supposes the antecedent stages but cannot be expected to follow them as a necessary consequence. In actual fact the character of the knowledge process as an example of a sequential order is generally recognized as far as the earlier stages and the very latest stage of the knowledge process are concerned. Between them lies an area usually called history where the flood of details available to enquirers tends to obscure from their eyes the developmental structure, the charac-teristics of a sequential order. With regard to the early stages of human knowledge development one can find some understanding of the fact that the knowledge and use of metal as the raw material of tools did not precede but followed the knowledge and use of stone. One is not unaware of the fact that the use of iron for human ends is more complex and requires a greater skill than the use of copper. The knowledge people gained while handling copper alloys such as bronze served as stepping-stones on the road towards the more difficult manufacture of iron tools.

Similarly one recognizes the sequential order of change in one's own time if one speaks of developing and developed countries. According to present fantasies only the period flanked by these two developmental ages has an entirely non-developmental or historical character. The present age itself, moreover, offers many easily accessible examples of different stages of a sequential order existing side by side or following each other in a diachronic sequence. An order of this type is not confined to knowledge. However, the development of human knowledge is a good example of this type of order. As one may see, it implies that humankind, seen itself as a process, replaces as the subject of knowledge the fictitious picture of a wholly autonomous and independent individual. Sooner or later the developmental character of the period we now call history, the period leading from Antiquity to pre-modern times, with all its ups and downs, may become visible. In this context a bird's eye view of the knowledge process may be enough to highlight gaps in our present knowledge at the empirical as well as at the theoretical level.

It is not easy to perceive the long-term knowledge process as a development, because among other things one possesses today, as a matter of course, knowledge such as that of the origin of infectious diseases, which was wholly inaccessible to a long line of generations before us. It is difficult for those who already know to reconstruct for their own understanding the conditions of those who did not yet know. This extension of one's imagination is needed for a fuller understanding of the knowledge process and of the characteristics of a sequential order.

An aspect of the growth process of knowledge which may easily be overlooked becomes more visible here. Attention has already been drawn to the fact that this process is uniquely human. The ability to transmit knowledge in the form of symbols from generation to generation is a crucial condition of the growth of knowledge. It enables a later generation to utilize knowledge without having to go through all the experiments and experiences which their ancestors needed in order to produce this knowledge. Normally one is not conscious of the fact that one's own ways of thinking and perceiving the world are steered into specific channels by the socially standardized language which one has made one's own and which one uses with ease as a matter of course. One can use language and knowledge as they are when one enters the community of the living and remain quite unconscious of the fact that into their making went the labour and the experience of generations now dead.

The term 'consciousness' itself can serve as example. As routinely used it does not seem to have a particularly close relationship with knowledge. On second thoughts, one may perhaps discover that the term consciousness is often used as if it referred to the form of which knowledge is the content. But the form of what? The conception which represents a human being as a kind of vessel, a container solidly separating something inside from the world outside, has taken deep root in languages such as English, French or German. It requires quite an effort of self-distancing to notice that the imagery is anything but self-evident and deserves closer scrutiny. That consciousness may appear as a kind of stage which exists prior to any experience or knowledge, or as a large room which can be filled with knowledge as a wine cellar may be filled with bottles of wine, is an illusion. 'We are conscious of ourselves' means in essence we have knowledge of ourselves. This is an example of the way in which symbols can lead one astray. There is no separation of content and form. No consciousness without knowledge, no knowledge without consciousness. Consciousness is merely another word for the condition in which stored sound-symbols, or in other words knowledge as a means of orientation, can be mobilized at will in the normal way. The Freudian term 'unconscious' refers to a condition in which stored experiences, though they may be still effective as determinants of action, cannot be recollected at will. Some experiences stored as part of one's knowledge cannot be remembered or can only be remembered with medical help.

The crucial question as to whether and how far socially standardized symbols correspond to the facts as they are must remain indeed doubtful and ultimately an unanswerable question. The reason is obvious. The world is immense. The idea that an individual person relying entirely on personal resources can acquire reality-congruent knowledge of this vast and complex world in which we live is an illusionary thought. Yet implicitly the ideal of an omniscient human being, of a person who knows the truth of everything, plays its part in many classical theories of knowledge. The image of a finite world which could be known to a person in its entirety underlies their arguments as a tacit assumption. It may be hidden behind such concepts as those of 'truth' or 'rationality'. It is the unspoken ideal underlying a stationary approach to the problem of knowledge which all mainstream philosophies share.

There were exceptions. The philosophies of Hegel and Comte are probably the best known. Both men were influenced by the experience of the French Revolution. Both tried to break away from the stationary character of the philosophical approach to knowledge and to replace it by a process model of knowledge. Both, each in his own way, tried hunting down the same problem. They presented models of the development of knowledge at a very high level of synthesis or, as we are used to saying, of abstraction. One may be inclined to suggest that they made attempts in the right direction. But Hegel and Comte made these attempts at a stage in the development of knowledge at which the empirical evidence available for a synthesis of this kind was still inadequate. Its gaps had to be filled by speculation. In that sense their attempts at reconstructing the development of knowledge were premature. The models they provided were marred by wishful thinking not kept in check by an adequate knowledge of details. The task they set themselves enforced in both cases a break with the tradition which presented as the subject of knowledge an isolated individual. Hegel, like Comte, saw in fact as the subject of knowledge a social unit, the chain of interlocking generations, even though he personified it as spirit or as *Geist*. It is far from accidental that the heritage they left had its greatest influence not in the field of philosophy, but in that of social science. Comte's work influenced Durkheim, Hegel's work Marx. During the nineteenth and twentieth centuries philosophers, in their theories of knowledge, largely returned to the individual-centred and non-processual tradition of Descartes and Kant. Hegel's and Comte's attempted break with that tradition was avenged by a fierce stigmatization. Among philosophers and, at a time when social scientists in such matters followed the philosophers' lead, among sociologists too, their works came to be outlawed and an object of scorn.

Meanwhile the social fund of empirical knowledge about the advance of human knowledge has grown and is growing rapidly while new attempts at a high-level synthesis are firmly discouraged by the disasters that have overtaken the work of earlier producers of syntheses, above all that of Hegel and Comte. The growing knowledge about details of the growth of knowledge was largely the work of historians whose professional training accentuates the provision of details from reliable source material while their professional ideology, since the days of Ranke, dismissed attempts at a higher-level synthesis as unsound. Thus the odds were against the making of such attempts. The human sciences were saddled with a heritage which blocked the road to a higher-level synthesis and thus theoretical models of long-term social processes.

Yet it is hardly possible to assess an individual's contribution to the growth of knowledge without reference to his or her point of departure within the overall growth of knowledge. In particular, the growth of natural sciences offers a striking example of a long-term social development, of an unplanned social process of long duration. There is much material, still largely unused, which can help towards a better understanding of the development of human symbols towards greater reality-congruence and thus of the meaning of this concept. A good deal has still to be learned and has to be unlearned before one can hope for a wider understanding of the fact that the sociologists' endeavour to provide testable models of long-term processes is in essentials quite different from the historians' approach to society. The latter can still proceed as if individuals were a beginning while the former are bound by the fact that even the greatest innovators continue. It is hardly possible to assess an individual's contribution to the growth of knowledge without reconstructing the social standard of knowledge which formed the innovator's point of departure. Methods of enquiring into not only the individual production of knowledge but also the changing standards of received knowledge from which producers depart, are still in the early stages of their development. The growth of natural sciences also offers examples of the fact that an individual's contributions to the growth of knowledge have the character of a continuation rather than that of an absolute beginning. An individual's dependence on a given fund of received knowledge can be very elastic. It is never absent. As humanity's fund of knowledge grows, by and large one can say that the individual's chances to innovate increase. The public reception of a discovery as such always involves other people. The historians' approach to the growth of human knowledge tends to accentuate the individual production of new knowledge and to underplay social reception. Yet without the latter an individual innovation lacks an essential aspect of a discovery.

Mapping out, for example with the help of textbooks, the changing social standards of knowledge in certain areas would also facilitate a testable type of synthesis. It would help in providing the kind of evidence needed for the production of fact-oriented process models in the field of human knowledge as well as in other fields. There are of course always limits to innovation. One can say that the discovery assumes the characteristics of knowledge only if it can be represented by symbols which are sufficiently standardized to be understood and scrutinized by others. Also one could make experimental assumptions about the direction of knowledge processes and look for evidence that contradicts or confirms them. The present scarcity of process models representing a high-level synthesis is to some extent justified. In the eighteenth and nineteenth centuries process models were often made on the basis of ideological preconceptions. There is no reason to exclude the possibility that such models could be made purely as instruments of scientific enquiries and as instruments of a more fact-related orientation of human beings in their world.

VIII

In all likelihood the evolutionary metamorphosis to communication by means of a language played a key role in the emergence of the distinctly human way of life. As one has seen, the transition to knowledge communication also opened the way to novel forms of orientation. It was an evolutionary innovation of great consequence. Familiarity with the use of sentences and words may make it difficult for us to perceive the fact. Perhaps it is only the comparison with the communication and orientation of animals where knowledge is at the most confined to a comparatively small orbit, which can make people, the descendants of animals, in full measure aware of the strangeness and uniqueness of a type of knowledge based on the learning of sound-symbols which may vary from society to society. We might refer to this fact more simply but also perhaps less accurately by saying: human beings communicate with each other and orientate themselves in the world by means of names they give to everything which appears relevant to their communication. It may well be that in olden days people were more aware of the fact that the power of naming all things in the heavens and on the earth was an exceptional asset of spirits and humans. Thus, in the Old Testament it is explicitly mentioned that God in creating darkness and light gave the name 'night' to the former and 'day' to the latter and that he left it to humans to give names to all animals.

As I have tried to explain earlier, humans can have knowledge of this world in two interconnected ways. They can have knowledge of events as a result of their personal, individual experiences involving their own sense impressions and they can have knowledge of events as possible objects of communication through sound-symbols representing them. They acquire these symbols and learn how to use them as components of a language. They can serve at the same time as means of communication and as a means of orientation. Without acquisition of a language humans cannot orientate themselves in their world. They cannot survive. Through the medium of a language human beings can acquire a great deal of knowledge of events of which they have no other personal experiences, involving sense impressions other than those made through the encounter with spoken or written words. On the other hand, knowledge which comes to an individual directly through the senses in the form of a personal experience here and now, never stands on its own. It is always thoroughly interwoven with sound-symbols that form part of a language and with knowledge acquired in the form of spoken or written words. Thus, one may touch a table and, if one closes one's eyes, make sure by means of a touch inspection all round that the object really is a four-dimensional object in space and time or, more specifically, a table. But by recognizing it as such one merely identifies an event of one's personal experience in terms of a communal social symbol, a particular position within the social universe of symbols and the fund of knowledge that goes with it. In that way a table can be said to exist as object of a human-made symbolic representation and as object in time and space. It would be a mistake to separate these means of localizing objects from each other or to treat them as incompatible. Present habits may make one's thought drift in that direction. However, as I shall have to explain in a short while, of all the things which have a place and a function in human communication nothing has ever a place in time and space alone without the representation in the form of a sound-symbol and nothing can have the character of a sound-symbol which is not also in time and space.

Every language contains classificatory systems as well as categories, models of relationships between events, real or thought to be real, and of the possible explanations of such events. By means of these categorial, explanatory and other models of connection the users of a language are enabled to determine symbolically the position of an individually experienced event within whatever it is they experience as their real world. In that way languages help their users to integrate and, generally, to organize individual perceptions in accordance with their position in this symbolic world. If at a given time a language does not provide a fitting classificatory or categorial niche, it may under certain conditions stimulate the development of a new symbol. Such an experience may stimulate the development of a new symbol which can appropriately harbour the experiences, not or not yet fitting the existing stream of symbols. The emergence of the word 'virus' can serve as example. The discovery of a previously unknown type of agents of illnesses would not have been a discovery if the new type of agents had remained without its symbolic representation. This discovery and the social processes which identified the newly found generators of illnesses symbolically with the sound-patterns 'virus' was specially designed to represent these agents in messages between human beings and thus at the same time to indicate their place in the speakers' world. In ordinary cases, such as that of the investigation of a piece of furniture, the person concerned might come up with a household word as a result of a personal inspection. An English-speaking person might conclude the investigation by saying: 'this is a table': while a German-speaking person would say that the object was a 'Tisch'. As one may see, human beings do not live in a four-dimensional, but in a *five-*

dimensional world. They locate objects of communication in accordance not only with their position in space and time, but also with their position in the speakers' own world as indicated symbolically by the sound-pattern which represents them in the speakers' language.

Perhaps it would be easier to recognize the high cognitive functions languages have for human beings if people were not so familiar with them. There may be something in the saying that familiarity breeds contempt. Might it not otherwise have been common knowledge and obvious that the languages which human beings speak have a fair share in fashioning their speakers' image of the world in which they live, including their image of themselves? They certainly have a determining influence on the outlook of small children who learn them as their mother tongue. They provide them with means of orienting themselves far beyond the field of their personal experience. Shall one regard this as a kind of biological or social a priori comparable to the natural a priori of transcendental philosophers?

There are many schools of transcendental philosophy which postulate a kind of natural a priori which interposes itself in such forms as the laws of reason or the laws of logic between the owner of that mind, between the individual subject of knowledge, and the world of which they seek to gain an accurate image. Though not always admitted, in that case human nature itself, the structure of the human mind, appears as the culprit which can never allow us to overcome the nagging doubt about the reliability of human knowledge, which interposes itself as an insurmountable barrier between subject and object, prior to any acquaintance the subject had with the object. One may come to the conclusion that the glittering garlands of words interposing themselves between subject and object of knowledge constitute a social parallel to the natural a priori of transcendental philosophy, but that is not the case. No doubt languages as factors of cognition can mislead as well as lead. Traditional equivocations may often outlive their usefulness for centuries in everyday languages with astonishing pertinacity. It is not particularly perturbing that the object–subject divide of philosophical epistemology has presented the English language with the gift of the antonyms subjective–objective, while in some contexts the term 'subject matter' can almost be used interchangeably with object.

What has been presented here as a form of symbolic representation may traditionally be presented as generalizations or abstractions. The underlying assumption seems to be that individuals first make their own experience with particular tables and then, after seeing several more of that kind, abstract from them the general concept 'table'. What actually happens in such cases is almost the opposite and decidedly more complex. This is another example of the difficulty many people experience in giving social data such as languages or knowledge their due as pre-existing any particular individual. Again thinking in terms of beginningless processes is required if one wishes to overcome this difficulty. One may be inclined to assume that the learning of a language by a young human child can be regarded as an absolute beginning. But that is not the case. Once more one has to refer to the fact that young children in their bio-social growing up process pass through a phase in which they by nature are readied to learn the language of those who bring them up. This is the hinge point in people's development which challenges most unmistakably the widespread belief that life in society runs counter to human nature. The biological process provides at this stage a natural disposition which can only bear fruit if it is activated by a social process, by older people who speak with each other and with the child, and by an individual learning process. On occasions culture battles against nature and nature against society, but it may be useful to remember once more that basic individual characteristics of human nature unfold themselves only through life with others, through life in society. The concatenation of a biological, a social and an individual process which is the condition of the human capacity to speak, is a vivid example of the interlocking of a biological, a social and an individual process at one of the turning points of a human life.

This is the key to an understanding of a relationship that is often misunderstood and it can do no harm to refer to it once more. Biological processes provide the potential for an individual's learning to speak and to understand a language. If this biological potential is impaired, as it may well be in a child which is deaf and dumb, a person may be unable to learn the audible form of a language. Also the child will not be able to learn and to understand speech if it is not cared for by a group of older people who speak a language with each other and with the child. The biological maturation process provides a child at a certain period with the disposition for learning to speak with others and to understand others. If at this period no other persons who care for the child speak with each other in its presence and speak to the child, the child's potential for learning a language at a later stage may be severely damaged. Here is most apparent what one may also observe on other occasions, that human beings are by nature made for a life with others, for life in a group. They are, in other words, by nature predestined for life in society and for entry into the symbol world as well as for life as a distinct individual with a voice of its own.

The habitus of our age produces a strong tendency to treat as opposed to each other what we perceive as different. We tend to think in terms of either-or. We ask: is language nature or culture? Maybe this tendency towards polarization in thinking mirrors an age of conflict and war. Whatever the reason, the example of language demonstrates that this tendency towards polarization obscures the question: what is the relationship? In this case the question is: what is the relationship between the natural, social and individual level of language? The sound component of language is present even in silent forms of using language such as thinking. Sooner or later the results of the silent form must be restored to an audible or visual form accessible to others. The natural disposition to speak is patterned and structured by a language shared by a multitude of people who form with each other a language community. Thus activated it serves the individual member of such a community to represent, to express, to orient itself. Rolled into one, natural, social and individual processes play a part in producing the symbols of a language.

By learning a first language, a mother tongue, children gain entry into the symbol world. They open up for themselves the chances of acquiring more knowledge, more symbolized experiences. But the language one learns as a child also limits — it may even block — the opportunities for making experiences, for acquiring knowledge. Children may for a while experiment with sound-patterns of their own until they learn which sound-patterns symbolically represent specific objects of communication for other people as well. They learn as their mother tongue the language of a *particular* society which existed before they themselves entered the world. It opens the door to the symbol world in a highly selective and thus in a limiting manner. It is possible that the manner in which human beings acquire access to a language is partly concealed from us by the unspoken assumptions represented by our language itself. It is not usual to say that small children learn the language of a particular society. It is usual to say that children learn to talk. In that way the acquisition of a language is made to appear a purely individual achievement. Attention is turned away from the interlocking of biological, social and individual processes that one encounters here.

The learning of an existing language implies that children's experiences are patterned by conditions which exist prior to their own existence. But these conditions, far from locking up or damaging the possibility to acquire knowledge of this world as it really is, are essential to the reality-congruence of their communication and orientation. The philosophical doubt about the possibility of reality-congruent knowledge is contradicted in a very elementary form by the success of the human species in its struggle for survival. If humans' cognitive endowment were really of a kind which did not allow them to recognize objects as they really are they would have gone under. The assumption of a congenital defect, which eternally casts in doubt the human capacity to recognize the world as it is, is inherently improbable. Humankind would soon have disappeared after developing such a defect. Instead they have gained for themselves a position of dominance over other species. This suggests that the means of orientation with which they are endowed are more effective, provide opportunities for greater reality-congruence of knowledge than those of most other living creatures. In fact, orientation by means of intergenerationally accumulated and expanded knowledge is probably the best, the most efficient of the various techniques of orientation with which living creatures have been endowed by the blind evolutionary processes of nature. It is odd, and has yet to be explained, that philosophers find a hearing for doctrines which suggest a congenital defect of the human means of orientation. It implies eternal uncertainty as to whether the sound-symbols of their languages can ever be made to represent accurately the various aspects of this world or even whether anything outside the enquiring individual really exists.

IX

I have tried to indicate the twofold character of our experienced world, as a world independent of, but including, ourselves and as a world mediated for our understanding by a web of human-made symbolic representations predetermined by their natural constitution, which materializes only with the help of processes of social learning. It can become more and can become less reality congruent. We can experience this world and ourselves within it here-and-now directly as a tangible entity, as a moment in a condition of change usually represented today as a process in the four dimensions of time and space. But it is also always represented by sound-symbols. If it were not symbolically represented human beings could neither know it nor communicate about it. In that sense one has to speak of a five-dimensional universe. By means of sentences and words people can refer to the world as it was, as it is, or as it may be in the future. In that case human beings can free themselves from bondage to the moment. Everything which can become an object of human communication can be located as an item in time and space and as an item of language or knowledge.

It is difficult to think of a single physical model of this constellation. Languages are quite unlike that which they symbolically represent except if they symbolically represent symbols. They constitute a layer of the human world which is unique. A sound-symbol can be mainly reality congruent or mainly a phantom with numerous shades and grades in between. Expressed differently, a language symbolically represents the world as it has come to be experienced by members of a society where it is spoken. One of the singularities of this layer is, therefore, that it reflects the world at large and at the same time the group of people, the societies which use the symbols as means of communication. Another singularity is that all the symbols imply relationships. They indicate how the people who use a particular symbol layer connect the world and its various aspects and items with each other. The items in a symbol layer are not absolutely unconnected and independent. Whether absolutely independent events exist in the world at large is a different question and one beyond my competence. But it is perhaps useful to say that language connects. You cannot say 'butterfly', 'handkerchief', 'yesterday', or 'it seems to me' without placing each of these items into a specific context.

Moreover, the web of relationships into which events are placed if they are represented in terms of a language, is never the product of short-term experience alone. Every language is an heirloom, the product of an incalculable sequence of generations. Individual members of a society using a common language can enrich it or misuse it, but the power individuals have to alter it is limited because it is one of the main functions of a language to make communication possible among a multitude of people, and because an individual alteration would make understanding difficult if not impossible if it diverged too much from the standardized sound-symbols of a language. A language has in relation to every individual who uses it a power of its own. Although in some societies no doubt individuals are free to use the common language in whatever way they like, one may perhaps underrate the extent to which the web of standardized symbols of a common language through which every person looks into the world affects what one wishes to say or what one can say.

One may not be aware of the fact that the sound-patterns of a language have the character of an agreed symbol or object of communication. No social contract was signed which made the sound-pattern 'nature' a symbol of almost everything not made by humans. In most cases the sound-symbols of a language grew into their present shape through the use of these or similar sounds as symbols of specific objects of communication through the social practice of communicating with others. Sometimes an academy gains the power to determine the usage of words. Sometimes a dictionary acquires this function. There are cases in which social groups such as a court society or a city patriciate have a model-setting influence upon the use of language; the fortunes of that group determine the fortunes of its languages.

Models of the relationships between three basic elements form the hard core of all theories of knowledge, between those who know (the subjects), that which they know (their knowledge), and that of which something is known (the objects). As one may have seen, the working model of the three basic elements and their relationships which has been presented here differs from that used in traditional theories of knowledge. In the case of the latter the nature of knowledge itself remains essentially unclear. It is usually conceived as something within the head of people, as distinct from the world outside: an idea, a conception, a thought, or perhaps something a person said, a judgement or a statement. This spatial imagery, the location of knowledge *within* the head of a person, is often combined with the description of knowledge as part of a science. A science, however, is a social fact. It presupposes intergenerational relationships embracing co-operation or disputes. Yet, how the location of knowledge within a single head and in pronounced distinction from all that is outside, can be combined with its mode of existence as part of a social unit, of a science, is perhaps not too clear. The question of the ontological status of the language-knowledge complex is open. There seems to be a tacit agreement that knowledge is something immaterial. But the question of how a science can be concerned with something no one can see, hear, touch or connect with any other sense experience, is hardly ever raised. At the same time people appear to differ with regard to the classification of knowledge as part of human nature or as part of culture. All in all the question of the ontological status of knowledge is hardly seen as a question of major concern and yet it does seem to have some bearing on the key question of knowledge, the question to which one refers in such terms as truth, validity or cognitive value. It has widely been accepted that knowledge was not a replica or an imitation of the world. The question of whether knowledge mirrored reality or whether it was a picture of reality has often been discussed. But on the whole the uncertain status of knowledge is widely taken for granted as one of those things not worth bothering about.

In this text, as one has seen, knowledge has been closely identified with language and language with knowledge and thought. This removes one of the sources of uncertainty. It includes possible extensions such as the language of mathematics, specialized sets of sound-symbols not automatically included if one uses the term 'language' in its standardized form. They all have *communication functions* as well as *orientation functions*. In fact it is difficult to think of any language utterance which does not combine these two functions. I have tried to show in some detail that the symbol function of sound-symbols need not be impaired if their sound component is kept silent. The term 'knowledge' is often used with reference to a voiceless use of chains of sound-symbols. That the sound-symbols of languages can be stored, remembered and manipulated in a voiceless form has contributed to the impression that knowledge and language are two different and separately existing human manifestations. Handling sound-symbols silently certainly diminishes their communication function and emphasizes their orientation function. But in the end knowledge can fulfil its orientation function only if the voice, and thus its communication function, is brought back to life. Sooner or later knowledge has to assume its sensory form as a spoken or written communication of a person with other persons.

Languages have been presented here as a layer of the human world. One cannot understand their mode of existence as long as the differentiation of basic concepts such as nature and culture, societies and individuals is not counterbalanced by the qualification of their relationships, by instruments of synthesis. Language and knowledge are examples of the latter. They are inseparable. Human beings cannot communicate without handling knowledge, nor handle knowledge without use of a language, without sooner or later communicating with others. There is thus a very pronounced difference between the level of synthesis at which the older theories explore the problem of knowledge and the level of synthesis to which this exploration is geared. In order to determine the relationship between language and knowledge a unitary frame of reference is needed. This is provided here by the recognition that both language and knowledge are functions of symbols. On the face of it knowledge is set apart from language. One can translate knowledge from one language into another. This seems to indicate an existence of knowledge in separation from that of language. It is easy to overlook the fact that translation does not imply the removal of knowledge into a realm without language. It refers to the possibility of changing knowledge from the set of symbols of one society to the set of symbols of another. Up to a point the same message can be conveyed by different sets of sound-symbols.

Traditional theories of knowledge are concerned with scientific knowledge only; they are only marginally interested in human knowledge prior to AD 1500 and in non-scientific knowledge at a later stage. Yet there is a good deal of evidence which suggests that the growth of pre-scientific knowledge was a condition of the emergence of the scientific form. Ptolemy's error was a condition of Copernicus's correction of this error. The separation of scientific from pre-scientific knowledge condemns theories of knowledge to sterility. The obvious aim is a unitary theory embracing all types of knowledge. The present enquiry is a step in that direction; it prepares the way for models of the long-term process of human knowledge which, without any absolute beginning, goes back to an unknown sequence of evolutionary stages. One can only surmise that communication by means of learned languages and orientation by means of learned knowledge emerged in stages, as novel evolutionary techniques from communication by means of unlearned signals and orientation — by what we call inborn instinct. We do not know how, why and when. We only know the result, a spectrum of knowledge ranging from communal fantasies to reality-congruence with many shades, grades and blends between them.

Seen without the evolutionary context, fantasy knowledge and reality-congruent knowledge may appear merely as polar antagonists. It is only by presenting them in their evolutionary context that one becomes aware of the kinship between fantasy knowledge and reality-oriented knowledge as manifestations of the same evolutionary stage. One may recognize the latter as the distinguishing characteristic of human beings and overlook the fact that transmissible fantasy knowledge also forms such a characteristic. Apes may act upon fantasies when young, but their games are genetically determined and identical throughout a species of apes. Human beings alone, as far as is known, have the gift of regulating behaviour in accordance with fantasy knowledge which is not innate though it may fashion innate desires, and which has been individually acquired through learning. Their culture is to a large extent derived from this gift. Given the limits of our evidence one can say that no zero point of either fantasy knowledge or reality-congruent knowledge is imaginable in groups of hominids of the only surviving type.

At the earlier stages of humanity's course of life the scope of reality-congruent knowledge, in many respects much more detailed than ours, was unavoidably more limited. Fantasy knowledge, as I have indicated before, at that stage had a high survival value for human beings. Myth closed the gaps of their realistic knowledge. It protected them from the horror of having to know how much they did not know.

Although reality-congruent knowledge has gained the upper hand in many of the more developed societies of our age, fantasy knowledge continues to play a part in human behaviour. Although the latter usually predominates in less developed societies, there is never a zero point of reality-congruent knowledge. An integrating perspective reveals as a fact, not as a desideratum the structure of the movement. I have alluded to it before. It is relatively simple and goes hand-in-hand with a change in the subject of knowledge. A theory of knowledge which is focused on the knowledge function of sound-symbols requires as the subject of knowledge, not alone this or that human person, but human societies in their development and ultimately the development of humanity. If that is understood the much debated but previously unanswerable question of the possibility of reality-congruent knowledge admits a clear and testable answer. With the process of humanity as the social framework it is not difficult to show that the balance between fantasy knowledge and reality-congruent knowledge, in an intergenerational context *can* change in favour of either, but in the case of knowledge of non-human nature *has* in fact changed in favour of reality-congruence. Both types of knowledge may develop into social specialisms such as science on the one hand, the arts, religion and some other cultural attainments on the other.

The example indicates why I have chosen the concept 'reality-congruence' as symbol of one of the types of knowledge. One used to speak without hesitation of the truth of a statement. But 'truth' has strong moral undertones. One of its most obvious antonyms is 'lie'. Yet it would be misleading to call a lie every scientific statement which in the course of the development of a science reveals itself as untrue. Also 'truth' is often misunderstood as similarity or identity of statement and fact, of the constellation of symbols of which a statement consists with the facts which it represents. The symbol character of statements makes it easier to understand why 'congruence' has been chosen in order to characterize the relationship between symbol and that which it represents. It indicates the representational character of the sound-symbol which in a given language stands for a specific sound-symbol or a combination of such symbols.

As long as knowledge was seen as essentially insubstantial, as something of the 'mind', one probably could not go further in clarifying this relationship. If the character of knowledge as a symbolic representation of objects of communication is taken into account and thus also its character as socially stamped sound-patterns, deposited in people's memory tracts, the tacit body–mind dualism colouring many discussions about knowledge as an unspoken assumption disappears. The interpersonal aspect of knowledge is brought more sharply into focus. The relationship between interpersonal messages with a knowledge function, spoken, written or stored in memory, and the object of communication reveals itself as the relationship between constellations of symbols and that which they symbolically represent. Representational concepts of this type lack the stationary character of absolute finality which tradition has associated with concepts such as 'truth'. The expression congruence used in this manner can indicate the direction of a movement. It admits shades and grades. One constellation of sound-symbols can be more and can be less reality congruent than another. But the transformation of languages with the long tradition of process-reducing formulas, of representing events in stationary terms, into languages fit for the symbolic representation of processes, is certainly not a simple task. It may take a very long time.

It is sometimes argued that only since the coming of science in the sixteenth and seventeenth centuries of our era can humans be said to possess the means of acquiring true or valid knowledge of nature. They give the impression that scientific knowledge came into being as a result of the accidental appearance in Europe of a number of unusually gifted individuals. In actual fact the breakthrough to what we now call a scientific form of acquiring knowledge of nature would have been impossible and must remain quite incomprehensible without the antecedent advances in knowledge made in Antiquity and the Middle Ages. Even those of our ancestors who spent their lives as hunters and food gatherers or as early agriculturalists possessed a great deal of knowledge which, though one cannot call it scientific, certainly deserves to be called reality congruent. It deserves this characterization even though it was blended throughout with dominant fantasy knowledge.

At present the ability to perceive long-term processes encompassing thousands of years, such as the growth of humankind's knowledge of nature, is seriously impaired by the historical mode of perceiving and presenting the human past. This mode of perceiving the past not only suggests an often artificial break between what is called prehistory and history, it also focuses attention to such an extent on details, that process structures which demand a long-term vision may be theoretically disregarded. If the development of humankind as a whole is used as a frame of reference, the growth of reality-congruent knowledge is indeed obvious. Although many details of that type of knowledge once possessed by members of simpler societies are now lost, humankind's overall fund of knowledge has grown over time at both the empirical and the integrating theoretical levels. With it has grown the rule of humans over their fellow creatures on earth. Orientation with the help of knowledge has given human beings a great advantage over almost all other species. Perhaps one can explain the constancy with which object-congruent knowledge increased as a sign of its high survival value.

This is not to say that the process of knowledge growth has uniformly gone in the same direction. A more detailed survey would show a rather complex pattern of advances in knowledge intermingling with blockages and regressions. I can briefly mention as an example four stages in the development of Middle-Eastern and European knowledge as a continuous process whose earliest known stage was the development of visual symbols, in other words writing, in addition to audible symbols, in other words spoken language, as means of communication in ancient Sumer. One can distinguish two distinct phases of priest-dominated knowledge and two equally distinct phases dominated by secular groups:

> *First phase of priest-dominated knowledge* (c. late fourth millenium–sixth century BC).
> *First phase of secular knowledge* (c. sixth century BC–fourth century AD).
> *Second phase of priest-dominated knowledge* (c. fourth century AD–fifteenth century AD).
> *Second phase of secular knowledge* (c. fifteenth century AD —).

Comte's law of three stages comes to mind. However, the sequence briefly mentioned here is neither a law nor a model of a necessary and irreversible process. It is a purely fact-oriented model indicating one of the salient aspects of the continuity of knowledge transmission. It can be revised or abandoned if that is demanded in accordance with newly discovered knowledge of facts. The development of writing can serve as example of the continuity of knowledge development in spite of its transition from one people or one state to another. Whatever the descent of the Phoenician writing may have been, the Hellenic Greeks learned it from them. As far as we know it had no connection with the Mycenaean Greek alphabet which apparently was derived from an older form of writing developed in Crete. The Roman alphabet was one of the transformations of the Greek form of writing. The Roman writing transformed itself into the medieval writing and so into ours.

In Comte's time it was not unusual to include in the development of knowledge non-rational or religious knowledge as an early phase of knowledge development; he was not the only scholar of that age who suggested such a sequence as a quasi-natural necessity. At the end of the twentieth century one is in a better position to recognize that this was a fantasy. The scheme presented here indicates a close link between processes of knowledge and of state formation. The first flowering of priest-dominated knowledge was centred on the ancient Middle-Eastern monarchies of which those of ancient Sumer, ancient Egypt and Babylon are examples. In most of these states a priestly aristocracy headed by the chief priest and centred on the first large-scale social organization, on the temple household on the one hand and a warrior aristocracy headed by the king and centred on the palace on the other hand, were bound to each other as fellow rulers of the state and as rivals in many power struggles. Though in Egypt, more protected from invasions than the

Mesopotamian states during the earlier part of its history, the warrior aristocracy gave very early to an aristocracy of state officials engaged in a fluctuating power struggle with groups of priests. Although the groups centred on the palace made contributions to the development of knowledge, at that stage by and large priests dominated the production and transmission of knowledge.

A striking feature of the knowledge process comes to light if one compares the priestly organization and the structure of knowledge of the first priest-dominated phase with those of the second phase. The latter did not simply represent a return to the former. The advances made during the first period of secular knowledge were not simply lost in the second period of priest-dominated knowledge. The latter represented a complex blend of regression and progression. Myth ruled again where proto-scientific enquiry had ruled before. But the priestly organization modelled itself on the state organization of the Roman Empire which had given birth to it. In the form of a church it became much more highly centralized and unified than religious beliefs and cults had in the first phase of priest-dominated knowledge. One of its most significant innovations was its reliance on the authority of a book. The concept formation of the church benefited greatly from the advances in concept formation to higher level of abstraction or synthesis made at the preceding secular stage. In this context these examples may be enough to indicate that the four-stages model had in no way the character of uniform progressions and regressions. But they may at least illuminate the complexity of the knowledge process. The model invites comparisons. That is one of the criteria of its reality-congruence. It led to the emergence of a scientific form of discovery.

The example also illuminates the nature and function of models of long-term processes, in this case of long processes of knowledge growth. The advances in the natural sciences may tempt people to regard process models as a kind of law or of law-like generalizations. Comte succumbed to this temptation. But sociological process models have in no way the character of general laws for numerous recurrent special cases. The process represented by the four-stages model was probably unique. It may never happen again. This model provides an articulation of what I have said before, that a continuous process of knowledge transmission and growth can bind to each other the knowledge traditions of different countries and peoples. One can trace back to ancient Sumer the process of continuous knowledge transmission and growth which in the Renaissance blossomed forth in the form of scientific knowledge in what we now conceive as European countries. In the course of this process specific secular groups succeeded twice in breaking the monopoly over the transmission and production of knowledge that priestly groups had acquired before, first in Graeco–Roman societies and later again in European societies. In all likelihood the first spurt of secular knowledge and the absorption of some of its aspects by the second phase of priest-dominated knowledge was one of the conditions of the second secular spurt. Why was it, this is the problem, that in the context of the Sumero–European tradition secular groups twice succeeded in creating a knowledge tradition of their own and in gaining for their secular type of knowledge dominance over the priest-controlled knowledge? The characteristics which distinguish scientific and non-scientific knowledge can hardly stand out clearly if attention and factual knowledge is concentrated on the latter. I am raising the question here as an example of the role that models representing high-level syntheses can play in the study of human societies.

It may be useful if at the end I briefly point out two aspects of this study which are implied but which have not been made explicit. In at least two respects the empirical field of vision underlying the symbol theory is wider and the level of theoretical synthesis correspondingly higher than they usually are in historical, sociological and other social science studies. *First*, the implied social frame of reference of such studies is usually the main survival unit of our age, the nation state. It is in traditional anthropological investigations the tribe. That the state is the main level of integration to which enquiries are geared may not be as obvious in the case of sociological investigations as it is in historical investigations, but if one examines what sociologists mean when they speak of society one usually finds that they rarely go beyond the integration level of the state though they may confine their field of vision to sub-divisions of a state. Moreover, they usually confine their efforts to state-internal relationships. Sociologists rarely include in their field of vision, and thus in their conception of society, relations between states and the changes these undergo. In other words, the developments of continental groups of states and ultimately of humankind are as a rule regarded as lying outside the problem fields of sociologists. They are not so regarded here.

As long as society is implicitly identified with state-internal relationships between human beings, relations between states and humankind as the unit of integration they form with each other are made to appear as existing outside society or perhaps as not existing at all. In point of fact relations between states are relations between people. They are only different from family relationships and others within a state society in so far as they represent a different level of integration. They are no less real than social relationships below or at the state level. If nothing else, the use of violence in inter-state relationships, in other words wars, makes that very clear. That family relations, industrial relations and inter-state relations as subject matter for research belong to different academic specialisms may contribute to the impression that state-internal relations are social relations and relations at the inter-state level are not. If nothing else, the very obvious interdependence of different levels of society and the constant interdependence of their development could correct the impression.

The problem one encounters here draws attention to a gap in the conceptual armoury of sociologists with which they are not very well equipped to deal. Human societies, as they are constituted today, have several interwoven levels of integration. The kin group level, the tribal level, the state level, the continental level, and finally the level of humanity, they all are steps on the ladder. Observers of the contemporary scene may notice a very pronounced difference in the power chances available to representatives of different levels of integration at different stages of humanity's development. Sociologists and indeed social scientists in general are not yet adequately equipped to deal with human relationships at different levels of integration and with the developmental changes these can undergo.

A striking example is the transition from the tribal to the state level of integration that one can at present observe in parts of Africa. I have vivid memories of these changes. In the early 1960s I was teaching sociology at a Ghanaian university. I was invited to one of the great local festivals, and remember the set-up. It took place in the open air. The guests were seated in a very wide circle. The hosts, local chiefs, were seated at one side of the circle. At the opposite side was seated the guest of honour, the delegate of the state president. In their toga-like traditional costumes they looked like Roman senators, dignified and proud. The ceremony began with the chiefs getting up from their seats and walking with some of their followers slowly to the seats of the representatives of the state, presumably welcoming them to their festival. They returned to their seats. After a short interval the state representative and his staff got up and, walking through the whole circle, reciprocated the chiefs' visit, presumably thanking them for their invitation and expressing the good wishes of the head of state. What we saw was a symbolic representation of a certain equilibrium which had been reached in the long drawn-out tug-of-war between representatives of the two levels, of tribe and state. The president of the first African colony to become an independent state, while reserving more and more sources of real power for himself as head of state, wished to maintain as much as possible of the ceremonial power of tribal chiefs whom he regarded as a specifically African institution.

In details these processes of state formation may vary greatly. They can take the form of a hegemonic struggle for occupation of the state's governmental positions between different tribes or of a king's struggle with his powerful barons. Disintegration was usually the alternative to victorious integration at a state level. But many battles were usually fought before a final decision was reached. In Africa, too, the transition from the tribal to the state level often enough found its expression in war and destruction. The ceremony I witnessed indicated recognition of the supremacy of a state as well as recognition of the limited sovereignty of local chiefs. Analogous problems arise at the transition from the nation state to a continental federation of such states. They arise when superpowers put pressure on less powerful states. They arise too when superpowers in the name of humankind try to enforce rules to protect the individual against laws of his own state that they regard as inhumane. Struggles of this kind may well be the early stage of a long process in the course of which humankind as the highest level of integration may gain equality if not superiority of sovereignty compared with that of the state.

While in many parts of Africa the dominant integration struggle is still that between relationships at the tribal or village level and those at the state level, in other continents the dominant integration trend is the incipient movement from a nation state to a federation of such states. The transition from a multitude of European nation states to a union of European states is an example of this kind. Similar integration spurts in Latin America are still in the experimental stage. The nation state's supreme function as survival unit diminishes in an era of atomic weapons, supra-national economic markets and steadily shrinking travel time. Increasingly humankind as a whole emerges step-by-step as the most likely survival unit. This does not imply that the individual as a level of integration and unit of reference disappears. Just as in the Renaissance a pronounced spurt of integration at the state level went hand in hand with a loosening of the individual's bonds with traditional groupings such as kin group or guild, so in our days a spurt of integration at the level of humankind goes hand in hand with a strengthening of an individual's rights within the nation state.

At different stages of development different levels of integration stand out as the most powerful and effective. But in order to perceive these differences one has to stand back and to distance oneself from a many-levelled society and from one's own position within it. In the field of human societies scientific observers have to place themselves as it were at a different level of the spiral staircase from that of the objects they study. If one speaks of the state in the singular one stands at the level of a multitude of states. If one observes the multitude of states one tacitly stands at the level of humankind. No higher level of integration is available. For the sake of comparison, therefore, one chooses in this case antecedent levels of evolutionary integration. One tries to perceive the distinguishing characteristics of humankind by comparison with those of animals. By extending one's field of vision in this manner one ascends from the state to the plurality of states and thus ultimately to humanity as the tacit reference unit of sociological enquiries. If that is done the singularity of languages as means of human communication and of funds of knowledge as means of human orientation stand out more clearly. It is not unusual to speak of language in the singular when one actually refers to languages in the plural. In the case of knowledge the use of the singular can be justified by the supra-national identity of natural science knowledge and of technology. Yet different knowledge traditions exist side by side with this identical knowledge in different nation states. It is one of many languages, one of many knowledge traditions which children receive as their own.

What one observes as a fact, humanity's drawing more closely together, may help to support the theoretical point. In sociologists' work humanity, from being a distant ideal becomes a level of integration and a social formation among others. Both the theory of civilizing processes and the symbol theory can serve as examples. Evidence for both can be found at all levels of social development. All are stages in the development of humanity. The unit of comparison is always the span between the least and the most developed social units at a given stage. Ice-age societies and thus ice-age humanity in all likelihood nowhere transcended the tribal stage. Differences in their stage of development may elude us because at first approach and seen from a distance what remains from them all over the globe seems so much alike. The stage during which tribal units still had a chance to conquer an earlier type of city states and territorial states usually run by groups of priests and of warriors, lasted a few thousand years. Now a relatively small number of states swallow the tribes wherever they still exist.

Multi-dimensional models of human societies are needed in order to come to grips with the empirical evidence. The difficulty is that social scientists and sociologists in particular are still captives of a philosophical science theory which started with Descartes and took its cue from physics at that early stage of development. At that stage there was no need for multi-dimensional theoretical models. All objects of physics, and thus according to many philosophers all objects, seemed to represent the same and the only level of integration. Theoretical models of the type we call universal laws or generalizations were sufficient, and sufficiently reality-congruent to serve the requirements of physicists at that stage. These models have not lost their usefulness. But for some time now they have been supplemented even in the physical sciences themselves by theoretical models which, unlike laws, are multi-dimensional and which make it possible to handle experimentally data about objects such as large molecules, genes and chromosomes with several levels of integration acting and reacting upon each other.

An introduction to the symbol theory cannot be the place to explore the great variety of avenues into which one is led by the human capacity for symbolic representation. But a word of caution may be useful. The relationship between symbols and the objects they represent is not necessarily identical in all cases. In the case of language symbolization this relationship is different from that which one encounters in the relationship between theoretical models and the objects they represent. In the latter some similarity of structure is essential. In the case of language representation no similarity need be expected. This excursion may help to explain the sociologists' aim. One of the major aims is the production of testable models which enable people to understand better how and why societies function as they do and thus also what one may regard as their defects. They help to explain and thus also make accessible to a public enquiry the malfunctioning of societies. Sociological models, theoretical or empirical, are a means of experimentation and planned discovery. Both can have unexpected results. Sociological models, therefore, can also give rise to unplanned discoveries. One may perhaps regard as an open question whether the strong trend towards individual discontinuity of the models built by sociological theorists is compatible with the complexity of their task. Co-operation is not made easier by the fact that political doctrine often prevails over reality-congruence as the yardstick of a model's cognitive value. This may also help to explain why representation of societies as many-levelled structures is rare in sociological theories. Political doctrine is apt to limit the field of vision to intra-state issues. In actual fact intra-state issues can hardly be separated from inter-state issues: theories of society have to embrace both. Here the field of vision has been extended from the level of intra-state relationships to that of humankind.

Present custom highlights what language and knowledge at all stages have in common. It fails to supplement their common function and structure by a testable model of the changes they undergo. One may expect a single person — the 'great man' — to illuminate at one stroke in his work the great variety of problems which human societies present, but that is not a realistic expectation. This task cannot be performed single-handedly by one individual. It is a task which can only be performed by the co-operation of many individuals through a sequence of generations. It also requires, as I have already indicated, a widening of one's field of vision. One step in that direction has been taken here. A deep-rooted tradition which identifies society as society within a nation state has been challenged here. In the past the implied level of integration of the work of sociologists has often been neglected. Ultimately, in both cases, the frame of reference is humankind. This is one of the two extensions of the field of vision of which I have spoken. It implies above all, though by no means exclusively, a widening of one's vision of the contemporary scene. It accentuates the singularity of the only living beings who communicate with each other by means of languages and orientates itself as member of a specific knowledge tradition.

The *second* extension of the field of vision underlying the symbol theory concerns above all the extension of its framework into the past. One of the main characteristics of scientific knowledge is the planned extension of reality-congruent knowledge. As I have already said, before people reached the stage in which they aimed at a planned discovery they did not lack reality-congruent knowledge, but its acquisition, by and large, was haphazard and coincidental. Galileo and his successors discovered planned discovery by means of continuous sequences of model-building and systematically testing experimentation. But they could not have made their breakthrough to the planned discovery of reality-congruent knowledge without a great fund of reality-congruent knowledge which resulted from unplanned discoveries. A great mass of reality-congruent knowledge acquired more haphazardly by accident or good fortune was the condition of planned discovery.

In this context too it is fitting to use humanity as the social frame of reference. Our animalic ancestors did not have the distinguishing characteristics of humans as long as their main mode of communication was not that of learned languages and their main mode of orientation not that of orientation by means of learned knowledge. From early days on discoveries of high survival value travelled from the originating society to other societies. This enquiry suggests that one can distinguish between two stages in the emergence and growth of living beings who mainly communicate by using languages and who mainly orientate themselves by using knowledge, first in the form of audible, and later also of visible symbols. Both stages are hypothetical. But hypothetical models are better than a void. They facilitate discovery. The first stage is the evolutionary metamorphosis of animal species who communicate and orientate themselves mainly by means of genetically predetermined activities into an order of living beings we call humans, who perform the same activities by means of learned symbols. They have a genetically predetermined disposition for the use of these symbols which requires patterning through learning. The second phase mainly concerns the non-biological, intergenerational growth of humanity's language and knowledge traditions. This is a social or developmental process which in the early phases may have run side by side and may have intermingled with the evolutionary metamorphosis of ape-like animals into hominids of the present type. The social process is better documented than the biological process. But even in its hypothetical form the picture of the evolutionary branch of the humanization process articulates a problem which, answerable or not, social scientists cannot omit to raise if only as a means of clarifying the human image with which they work.

Two key questions are: how did humanity come into being? and what are its distinguishing characteristics compared with its more animalic forebears? If one speaks of the Palaeolithic or Neolithic age it is very much taken for granted that the social frame of reference is humankind as a whole. One often fails to see clearly that orientation with the help of a social fund of knowledge is one of the main characteristics which distinguishes humankind from other living beings. The search for properties which can help to explain differences in the make-up and behaviour of animals and those of humans are usually confined to differences in the properties of organisms seen alone as individuals and not yet also as societies. Bifocal vision and upright gait are examples. Best known and most popular are human distinguishing characteristics such as reason, mind, intellect or rationality. They all are concepts which support the ideal of the self-reliant individual, of an individual without group. They make one forget to observe as relevant differences in the manner in which animals and human beings live together, differences in their societies. And yet the latter, differences in their social life, are among the outstanding distinguishing characteristics of animals and humans. As I have already observed, animal societies can undergo great changes only as part of a change in their genetic make-up. Human societies can undergo great changes without any such changes in genetic make-up. At the root of many of these differences is the heightened capacity of humans for acting upon learned knowledge. It is this human condition which makes communication by way of languages and advances or recessions to a different stage in the development of societies, possible. The natural constitution of human beings prepares them for learning from others, for living with others, for being cared for by others and for caring for others. It is difficult to imagine how social scientists can gain a clear understanding of the fact that nature prepares human beings for life in society without including aspects of the evolutionary process and of the social development of humankind in their field of vision. This is the second extension of the field suggested here.

Extension with the accent on past and present times seems to demand supplementation by an extension of one's frame of reference into the future. However, social scientists are no prophets. But there are aspects of the future of humankind about which one can speak with reasonable certainty. In this respect I can offer an observation. It concerns the implied assumptions about the position of the present age within the development of humankind. The usual scheme with which we work — represented by concepts such as prehistory and history or Antiquity, Middle Ages and modern times — can easily give the impression that what we call modern times represents a relatively late stage in this development. Closely connected with it is the tendency to consider present times as a rather advanced stage in the development of human civilization. And if one considers the development of humankind in isolation this estimate is understandable. In this context it is not usual to extend one's field of vision to the development of the solar system. It is, however, not entirely without relevance for any estimate of the position of this age within the development of humankind. Life on earth and so the existence of humankind depends on the sun. Cosmologists inform us that the sun is at present at the middle of its foreseeable lifespan, as one might call it metaphorically, and that they expect the sun to continue its role as a life-supporting star for several thousand million years. If humankind does not destroy itself, if it is not destroyed by a meteor or another cosmic collision — which are certainly very real possibilities — the natural conditions of its existence will give humans the opportunity to tackle the problems of their life together on earth, or wherever, for a very long time to come. A future of 4000 million years should give humans the opportunity to muddle their way out of several blind alleys and to learn how to make their life together more pleasant, more meaningful and worthwhile. In the context of humanity's future, short-term perspectives are necessarily misleading. Today cosmologists appear to take it for granted that living creatures at the same level of development or even at a higher level exist elsewhere in the universe. I think one should not exclude from consideration the possibility that human beings owe their existence to a unique sequence of coincidences, that the development of human beings biologically equipped for the use of languages and knowledge is extremely rare, if not unique.

In the light of a future between the alternatives of self-destruction and a future of millions of years, the prevailing estimate which attributes to what we call modern times the character of a relatively late development demands correction. The fact that we have not yet learned how to curb wars, the reciprocal mass destructions of members of different states and other forms of behaviour that one cannot help calling barbarous, lends support to the assumption that in the overall context of the possible development of humankind what we call modern times represents a very early rather than a late stage of development. I like best the suggestion that our descendants, if humanity can survive the violence of our age, might consider us as late barbarians. I am not indulging in reproaches. Humans have to go through a long period of learning how to live with each other in peace. Our uncertainty, our inability to eliminate violence, are part of this learning process. No teachers are at hand. Outside help, evidently, is not forthcoming. Expressions of good will, exhortations to good behaviour, are welcome but hardly effective. The professing of antagonistic ideals inflames rather than tempers violence. People have to learn for themselves how to live with each other. In this case too planned discovery of explanations may be of help. As yet we do not know how to curb or how to eliminate violence effectively from human relations. We are trapped in a situation in which governments who are seriously concerned with eliminating wars also participate in and favour a flourishing arms trade which helps other nations to prepare themselves for war.

We have not yet learned to cope with the obvious contradictions of our age. We know already *that* human beings are able to live in a more civilized manner with each other, but we do not know *how* to bring it about in our life with each other, or at least only sporadically. We know already that much depends on achieving a better balance between self-restraint and self-fulfilment, but a stable social order that warrants such a balance still eludes us. It should not be beyond the reach of humanity in the thousands of years ahead of us.

Notes

Richard Kilminster has acted as editor of this paper. I am grateful to him. He has contributed much to whatever utility this paper may have. Obviously I alone am responsible for its weaknesses. The comments of Jan-Willem Gerritsen have been of great help to me and so has the continuous co-operation with my assistants Rudolf Knijff, Saskia Visser and Anne Gevers.

Reference

Huxley, Julian (1941) *The Uniqueness of Man*. London.